YOUR HIGH-PERFORMING VIRTUAL FAMILY OFFICE

YOUR HIGH-PERFORMING VIRTUAL FAMILY OFFICE

MAXIMIZING *Your* FINANCIAL *and* PERSONAL LIVES

RUSS ALAN PRINCE, VINCE ANNABLE, *and* ROBERT ANNABLE

▲VFO

VIRTUAL FAMILY OFFICE
ADVISORY GROUP

YOUR HIGH-PERFORMING VIRTUAL FAMILY OFFICE
Maximizing Your Financial and Personal Lives

FIRST EDITION

ISBN   978-1-5445-4422-9 *Hardcover*

978-1-5445-4423-6 *Paperback*

978-1-5445-4424-3 *Ebook*

CONTENTS

To Sandi,

For coming through in the most difficult times

Love, Russ

***

This book is once again dedicated to my father and mother, Robert and Madelon Annable, who told me my entire life growing up that I could achieve anything I set my mind to, and to my wife, Deborah, who never quit believing in me and to this day is my biggest supporter, and our five children, Matthew, Robert, Lauren, Jonathon, and Katelyn, because they always stuck with me in every pursuit of those goals and dreams. And to my precious grandson Rory, who provides us all with so much joy and entertainment.

And...

To our many faithful, valued clients who have trusted us with their financial and personal lives.

And...

To our VFO partners who believed in our vision to create The High-Performing Virtual Family Office they and our clients are experiencing now.

And of course...

To our in-house VFO Advisory Group team that keeps growing and allowing me to pursue the vision, Robert, Andrew, Lauren, Aaron, JT, Kyal, Mark, and Rynae, who have supported and worked tirelessly in the growth of The Virtual Family Office.

—Vince

***

INTRODUCTION

THIS BOOK IS A BRIEF INTRODUCTION TO ONE OF THE fastest-growing trends in the high end of the private wealth industry—the virtual family office. We wrote this primer for wealthy individuals and families who want superior results.

For our purposes, a wealthy individual or family has a net worth of $10 million or more. For pedagogical reasons, we are distinguishing the wealthy from the super-rich, which are families with a net worth of $500 million or more. Although the wealthy will likely turn to virtual family offices or some other version of a multifamily office, the super-rich will usually establish a single-family office.

The reason for this book is the same reason the wealthy are gravitating to virtual family offices. Generally speaking, the wealthy are being poorly served. While the super-rich, often through their single-family offices, are attaining superior results by getting the best, cost-effective solutions and not missing out on any meaningful opportunities, the wealthy cannot claim the same.

IS A VIRTUAL FAMILY OFFICE RIGHT FOR YOU?

As we will see, with a high-performing virtual family office, you can achieve the same advantages the super-rich attain from their high-performing single-family offices. In order to see if a high-performing virtual family is right for you, consider the financial and legal professionals you are relying on today.

Please rate the following ten statements using the following scale:

Not at all accurate　　**Extremely accurate**

1　2　3　4　5　6　7　8　9　10

_____ The financial and legal professionals you are working with really understand you as a person, including your hopes and dreams, concerns, and anxieties.

_____ The financial and legal professionals you are working with are very good at explaining complex concepts, ideas, opportunities, and solutions to you and to other people you bring into the conversation in ways you and everyone else clearly understand.

_____ You have a sincere and trusting relationship with the financial and legal professionals you are working with.

_____ The financial and legal professionals you are working with constantly and demonstratively put your interests way, way, way ahead of their own.

_____ You can consistently access best-of-class expertise and solutions for any issues you are dealing with—financial, legal, and otherwise.

_____ You can attain the expertise you and your family need and want on an exceptionally cost-effective basis.

_____ You can "go to the head of the line" when it comes to getting the services and products that will make a significant difference in your life and the lives of your loved ones.

_____ You are very confident you are not making any substantial legal or financial mistakes presently or with what you are considering doing.

_____ The financial and legal professionals you are working with extensively employ what-if thinking to identify possibilities and opportunities to determine the very best services and products for you to consider.

_____ The financial and legal professionals you are working with make sure you are staying on track and following the best possible course of action or ascertain whether certain alternatives would be more appropriate and effective.

Each 1, 2, or 3 rating indicates an important element that can very likely meaningfully help you achieve your goals or deal with concerns that are not being effectively addressed. A rating of 4, 5, 6, or 7 often means that the element is in progress but that you certainly could do better. When all the elements are rated 8, 9, or 10, you are likely working with outstanding professionals.

Ratings of 8, 9, or 10 are what the wealthy answer when they are working with high-performing family offices. Just consider:

- If your answers are not ALL 8, 9, or 10, what would happen if they were?

- How would your life be enhanced?

- How would your ability to take care of the people you love and the causes you care about be strengthened and enhanced?

If you engage a high-performing virtual family office, all your answers to these questions would be 8, 9, or 10.

EXPLAINING HIGH-PERFORMING VIRTUAL FAMILY OFFICES

Getting right down to it, this book is for you if you would like to—whenever possible—have the same financial and personal advantages as the super-rich. Because of their high-performing single-family offices, the super-rich very often achieve superior results. For instance, they are often able to get better after-tax investment performance. They can regularly ensure their wealth is not unjustly taken from them. They can create family dynasties where their fortunes and values perpetuate across the generations.

Do you want to work with an advisory firm that can deliver comparable exceptional value that high-performing single-family offices can deliver? If so, you may very well want to consider working with a high-performing virtual family office.

Due to advances in technology and some extremely clever professionals, a growing percentage of the advantages that were once exclusive to the super-rich are now available to the wealthy. This is increasingly the case because of the proliferation of high-performing multifamily offices, of which the high-performing virtual family office is one version.

With a high-performing virtual family office, you have access to the complete range of appropriate expertise available to the super-rich. Many of the services and products that work for the super-rich, however, you will never need. For example, if you do not have a billion dollars (or more) and want to protect a sizable portion of your wealth from maleficent entities, then the "floating island strategy" is not viable. If you do not have operating business interests in different jurisdictions, cross-border arbitrage strategies are not applicable. If you want to create a family dynasty leveraging a variety of different types of assets, including passion investments worth hundreds of millions of dollars, then you might consider laddered recombinant trusts; otherwise, this strategy is not for you.

We will be describing the world of family offices—both single-family offices and multifamily offices—in Part I. Critically, we will explain what makes a virtual family office high performing and why they have such a strong gravitational pull. More specifically,

- In *Chapter 1: What Is a High-Performing Single-Family Office?* we will introduce you to an obscure corner of the private wealth industry populated by the super-rich and their preferred provider.

- In *Chapter 2: What Are Virtual Family Offices?* we will explain the answer for the wealthy who want the advantages of a high-performing single-family office but cannot afford one.

- In *Chapter 3: What Makes a Virtual Family Office High Performing?* we detail the four factors that are essential for *any* family office to be high performing.

- In *Chapter 4: Why Do the Wealthy Increasingly Prefer Virtual Family Offices?* we examine the strong trend among wealthy individuals and families to choose virtual family offices over other types of providers.

As you read this book, think about what you want to accomplish. Recognize that a high-performing virtual family office may very well be the means for you to achieve your most important and meaningful financial and personal objectives, and it might effectively address some of your greatest concerns. We want to be open and say that a high-performing virtual family office is not for every wealthy individual or family. Therefore, we recommend, as you read this primer, that you think about the appropriateness of a high-performing virtual family office for yourself and your loved ones.

In Part II, we discuss some of the expertise that most successful business owners and other affluent individuals sometimes, if not often, fail to benefit from. We are only going to address a handful of targeted solutions you can potentially receive from high-performing virtual family offices. We intend to highlight some of the possibilities that are available and are often overlooked. Specifically,

- In *Chapter 5: What Is an Estate Plan?* we look at the components of estate planning from the basic to the more complex.

- In *Chapter 6: What Are Benefit-Focused Retirement Plans?* we detail a sophisticated qualified retirement plan that is very powerful for the "right" business owner but is not very well known among most professionals.

- In *Chapter 7: What Is Wealth Enhancement?* we describe some approaches to tax minimization which, unfortunately, many of the wealthy are overlooking.

- In *Chapter 8: What Is an Asset Protection Plan?* we discuss some of the ways you can avoid the pain of frivolous and unfounded lawsuits.

- In *Chapter 9: What Are Exit Strategies?* we talk about the different actions successful business owners can take to increase family wealth when they sell their companies.

- In *Chapter 10: What Are Alternative Investments?* we look at different types of investments beyond traditional stocks and bonds.

- In *Chapter 11: What Is Private Placement Life Insurance?* we discuss a solution regularly used by the super-rich to deal with taxes that is applicable to a large cohort of the wealthy.

- In *Chapter 12: What Is Concierge Medicine?* we describe a nonfinancial solution that is in high demand by the wealthy—getting the best healthcare possible.

Although we will be discussing specific services and products, you need to be cognizant of the fact that your high-performing virtual family office never sells. Only when one of these services or products is precisely appropriate are they introduced by professionals. Furthermore, even though we will discuss different services and products in Part II, if you are indeed working with a high-performing virtual family office, these solutions are regularly part of the mosaic and not a one-off service or product.

Again, high-performing virtual family offices are not for everyone, irrespective of the level of wealth. If you believe a virtual family office is right for you, we recommend you make a concerted effort to select a high-performing one and negotiate an arrangement that works for everyone.

Enjoy the book.

PART I

YOUR HIGH-PERFORMING VIRTUAL FAMILY OFFICE

CAN YOU BENEFIT FROM A HIGH-PERFORMING VIRTUAL family office?

For most of the wealthy, the preferred choice is vastly becoming a family office practice of some type, such as a virtual family office.

As we have said, a high-performing virtual family office is not for everyone. In some cases, it is much more than is necessary. In other cases, a high-performing virtual family office simply is not the best choice because the wealthy want only one service or product and they know precisely what they want.

High-performing virtual family office professionals can—based on their deep understanding of you and your world—provide the appropriate expertise that will enable you to effectively address a wide range of issues, needs, and wants. Essentially, a high-performing virtual family office will produce superior results.

1

WHAT ARE HIGH-PERFORMING SINGLE-FAMILY OFFICES?

FAMILY OFFICES ARE AT THE PINNACLE OF THE private wealth industry. This is because a large and growing percentage of the super-rich establish single-family offices. Simply put, the super-rich prefer to set up and run single-family offices rather than rely on a plethora of financial and legal professionals. In comparison to the alternatives, their single-family offices regularly produce superior results. For the wealthy, for whom a single-family office is not viable, a virtual family office can often provide them with the same superior results.

Single-family offices are not a new idea. We can track the concept back to about the sixth century when each member of royalty had a steward who was central to running the estate, including the household, the lands, and very often, the commercial enterprises. Furthermore, the stewards acted as managers and fiduciaries over the royal members' assets when the royals were away.

Even though we can date the concept of the family office to the sixth century, the concept of a family office is probably substantially older. The very wealthy relying on trusted servants likely goes back to when the very wealthy had trusted servants.

J. P. Morgan, Andrew Carnegie, and John D. Rockefeller meaningfully updated the concept of the family office with their single-family offices. These tycoons created separate corporate entities whose purpose was to manage their wealth and deal with a range of family matters. Since this time, single-family offices have proliferated very much in lockstep with the number and wealth of the super-rich.

Today, a single-family office is a separate legal entity whose aim is to maximize the financial and personal lives of family members. Before we dive into what a traditional single-family office commonly provides, let us look at how single-family offices are evolving and, at its core, what a family office is.

TYPES OF SINGLE-FAMILY OFFICES

Today, there are various types of single-family offices. The **traditional single-family office** is a separate entity built to meet the objective of a single family. It usually provides a range of services and products (see below) and is usually managed by one or more professionals. For the most part, the traditional single-family office is what people are talking about when discussing single-family offices. However, traditional single-family offices are no longer the only type of single-family office:

- An **embedded single-family office** often performs many of the functions of a traditional single-family office. However, it is not a separate legal entity as it is usually part of a family business.

- A **hub-and-spoke single-family office** is several separate legal entities intended to mitigate the cost of shared services while enabling different family members to take control over certain family office functions, such as investment management. There is a core single-family office responsible for a range of expertise that is available to all family members. This is the "hub." Then the different family members have added other expertise to their single-family offices, such as wealth planning and lifestyles services—these are the "spokes."

- In contrast to a traditional single-family office, a **limited single-family office** provides a relatively small number of services to the wealthy family. Most often, these single-family offices are only managing the monies of the wealthy family.

- Some professionals have expanded the definition of a single-family office beyond a single family. When several smaller (as measured by assets managed) single-family offices responsible to different, unrelated wealthy families combine resources, we have a **single-multifamily office**.

- A **communal family office** is where a single-family office is created for a group of closely aligned nonfamily members such as a religious organization. The family members are not related by blood, but they see themselves as one family.

There are many ways the super-rich and professionals discuss the concept of a single-family office, but at its core, a single-family office is very basic:

A single-family office is a coordinator of expertise that maximizes the lives of family members.

This means single-family offices are likely to provide different expertise to different wealthy families depending on the needs, wants, concerns, and preferences of the super-rich family members. Consequently, single-family offices are quite diverse in structure, operations, and deliverables.

The same is true of virtual family offices. They are coordinators of experts. In this way, they are able to deliver the appropriate level of expertise to the wealthy as if each wealthy family had its own single-family office.

There are single-family offices that are very lean operations relying on an extensive network of specialists to address the needs, wants, and preferences of family members. For example, one single-family office we worked with oversees approximately US$11 billion and has only four employees—a chief investment officer, two coordinators of specialists, and an office manager. This single-family office extensively outsources to external experts.

At the other end of the spectrum is a single-family office responsible for about $200 billion with a staff of 150. This single-family office has its in-house investment banking team, sixteen-person legal department, and forty-one-strong personal security division. Although this single-family office does occasionally rely on external experts, most of the expertise is delivered by employees.

The degree to which a single-family office makes use of in-house or external experts is correlated with the wealth and preferences of the super-rich family. The complexity of family and business matters coupled with a preferred level of control usually determines the extent to which a single-family office outsources.

We now turn to what a traditional single-family office tends to provide. As we have just discussed, each single-family office is designed around a particular family, so what each single-family office offers can vary extensively.

EXPERTISE PROVIDED BY A TRADITIONAL SINGLE-FAMILY OFFICE

Overall, traditional single-family offices tend to provide two major categories of expertise—wealth management and family support (Exhibit 1.1). Wealth management consists of investment management and wealth planning. Family support tends to include administrative and lifestyle services and special projects.

Exhibit 1.1: Expertise Provided by Many Single-Family Offices

WEALTH MANAGEMENT	FAMILY SUPPORT
Investment management • Discretionary investment accounts • Alternative investments • Passion investments **Wealth planning** • Income tax planning • Estate planning • Business succession planning • Asset protection planning • Charitable tax planning • Cross-border planning • Life management planning	**Administrative services** • Tax compliance • Bill paying • Financial statements **Lifestyle services** • Concierge medicine • Family/personal security • Philanthropic advisory **Special projects** • Adoptions • Buying an island • Overseeing the construction of a house • Aircraft acquisition • Overseeing family construction projects

These are umbrella categories often encompassing several different services and products. There are various ways to manage money as there are various subcategories of wealth planning. The same is true of the three types of family support services.

Let us dig a little deeper into each of the categories.

Investment management is core to many single-family offices. There are discernible patterns when it comes to what single-family offices invest in. Stocks, bonds, and real estate are common in the investment portfolios of many single-family offices. Various types of alternative investment funds (see Chapter 10) are also fairly common. Direct investing in private companies is characteristic of more and more single-family offices. But these patterns can change easily as social, economic, and family circumstances change.

Some single-family offices, for example, are heavily invested in passion investments such as artwork, numismatics, and antiques. At one single-family office we worked with, one-third of the investable assets are in precious stones, one-third in alternative investments, and the rest in US Treasuries. Another single-family office built an underground vault to store more than 2,000 rare coins and a small mountain of gold and platinum bars. Other single-family offices are investing and sometimes taking equity positions in hedge funds. Cryptocurrencies and blockchains are becoming popular investments at more and more single-family offices. Most single-family offices are open to just about all legally sanctioned possibilities.

Wealth planning often enables the super-rich to legally mitigate taxes as well as protect their assets. It is also instrumental in enabling the super-rich to ensure the continuity of the family fortune. The following are the most common specialties within wealth planning:

- **Estate planning** involves using legal strategies and financial products to determine the future disposition of current and projected assets.

- **Marital and related relations planning** entails planning for disruptions in the relationships between spouses and other lovers with the intent to protect the super-rich family's wealth.

- **Business succession planning** principally deals with tax-efficiently transitioning businesses to others, whether they are family or not.

- **Asset protection planning** entails employing legally accepted concepts and strategies to ensure that a super-rich family member's wealth is not unjustly taken from him or her.

- **Charitable tax planning** enables tax-efficient philanthropy.

- **Cross-border and inbound planning** is for super-rich family members who are operating businesses in different countries or are moving to different countries to facilitate business opportunities and minimize the taxes that are owed.

- **Life management planning** addresses an array of concerns from a wealth management perspective, such as how to best structure wealth to deal with the aims and issues of extended longevity.

When it comes to **administrative services**, the single-family office is the chief financial officer of the super-rich family. Administrative services tend to be very straightforward and mechanical but often serve a critical role. They include:

- Dealing with all tax compliance matters, including filing tax returns, audit defense, estate, and gift tax execution, tracking, and administration

- Developing and updating the family balance sheet

- Producing income and cash flow statements

- Providing budgeting plans

- Bill paying and expense reporting

- Tracking and reporting investments, including addressing cost and tax basis

- Bookkeeping

Lifestyle services are nonfinancial and nonlegal services that benefit the family. Of great concern to most of the super-rich is healthcare. This concern often translates into connecting super-rich family members with exceptional concierge medical practices and overseeing the ongoing relationship (see Chapter 12).

Family security is also very important to super-rich families. Family security firms provide a range of services such as personal protection services, cybersecurity, investigations, and due diligence.

Philanthropic advisory is when experts are engaged to help super-rich family members think through the charitable causes and organizations they want to benefit. Commonly, philanthropic advisory deals with what charities to support and often includes monitoring how gifts are used and their subsequent impact.

Special projects refer to one-off project management. Special projects are a catch-all category for work done on behalf of a super-rich family that does not fit into any of the other categories. Some examples of special projects include:

· Facilitating an adoption from another country

· Buying an island

· Overseeing the construction of a 60,000-square-foot mansion

· Arranging the paperwork and facilitating the process for admission to a private club

The ability of high-performing single-family offices to deliver exceptional results in these areas or others is predicated on the elite team of specialists they have either on staff or who are readily available.

CONCLUSIONS

For a large and growing percentage of the super-rich, the answer is a single-family office. They are the most effective means for the extremely wealthy to maximize their financial and personal lives.

What is important to note is that as the number of the super-rich continues to multiply and the wealth they control continues to incredibly expand, the number of single-family offices will continue to multiply. Additionally, new types of single-family offices will appear. Even though we have described what traditional single-family offices tend to deliver to their super-rich families, more and more the offerings are highly customized.

With this chapter as a brief high-level overview of single-family offices, we now turn to virtual family offices. By understanding the single-family office of the super-rich, you will see how you can get the same advantages of the super-rich by engaging a virtual family office.

2

WHAT ARE VIRTUAL FAMILY OFFICES?

SINGLE-FAMILY OFFICES ARE ESTABLISHED TO SERVE one super-rich family. Of late, some variations tend to stretch the definition of one family. Multifamily offices, in contrast, are in the service of a handful to a large number of wealthy families. Interestingly, multifamily offices—that is, those professionals claiming to be a part of a multifamily office—are increasing at a faster rate than the number of wealthy families.

The wealthy, more and more, prefer to depend on multifamily offices compared to other kinds of providers such as wealth managers and accounting firms. The ability of multifamily offices to deliver holistic and synergistic solutions makes them the preferred advisor to the wealthy. The fact that multifamily offices are dominating the private wealth industry has not gone unnoticed by financial professionals. Consequently, an ever-growing number of these other types of professionals are claiming to have family office practices of one kind or another.

Just as there are different types of single-family offices, there are different types of multifamily offices.

TYPES OF MULTIFAMILY OFFICES

To be clear, a multifamily office is a family office, which means it is a ***coordinator of expertise***. How multifamily offices are organized and how they focus their capabilities results in different types. When a family office is "high performing," it is able to optimize the financial and nonfinancial lives of the wealthy.

A **virtual family office** is a bespoke arrangement where several professionals and other providers are coordinated by one or more professionals on behalf of several or more wealthy individuals and families. The aim is to mirror the bespoke nature of a single-family office as closely as possible.

There is a meaningful but nuanced difference between a traditional multifamily office and a virtual family office. The former tends to have a much broader set of in-house specialists. In contrast, with a virtual family office, some of the expertise comes from the professionals coordinating the virtual family office, but the majority of the services and products are provided by external experts. By design, virtual family offices tend to extensively outsource to selected specialists.

What is usually considered a **traditional multifamily office** provides a suite of deliverables characteristic of a traditional single-family office to a number of wealthy individuals and families. In most cases, multifamily offices are an extension of the wealth management model. The aim of these firms is often to work with fewer but wealthier clients. At traditional multifamily offices, certain expertise such as investment management is in-house and it often generates a substantial amount of the firm's revenues.

A **family office practice**, in contrast, is a professional firm providing its expertise, and mostly only its expertise, to a wealthy individual or family. The services and products provided are usually a subset of what a single-family office would often provide.

However, there are many accounting firms, for example, delivering tax services including tax planning, bill paying, financial statements, and so forth that refer to this group in their firm as their family office practice. Some investment managers, for instance, focus 90 percent of their energy on managing money and 10 percent on other client matters, yet refer to themselves as a family office or, more commonly, claim to have a family office practice.

Most family office practices are delivering a small set of expertise compared to what a single-family office might provide, but this is rapidly changing. With the ability to build elite teams of specialists, many family office practices are looking more like virtual family offices. The terms "family office practice" and "virtual family office" are becoming interchangeable with the former mirroring the latter.

ADDITIONAL EXPERTISE IN MANY VIRTUAL FAMILY OFFICES

In the previous chapter, we discussed what traditional single-family offices tend to provide to the super-rich. A great many virtual family offices commonly provide the same menu of expertise such as investment management and wealth planning. However, they provide additional types of expertise as well. This is a function of the nature of their wealthy clients. The following are some examples of these additional forms of expertise. This list is meant to be representative rather than exhaustive.

Family Governance Services

Leaving the family business to heirs can be complicated. Many times, doing so is plagued by interpersonal conflicts that can destroy the business and the wealthy family. Convincing a wealthy family to work cooperatively can be fraught with problems. A high-performing virtual family office has the expertise to foster family cohesiveness.

Effective family governance often starts with delineating the wealthy family's history and values. Sharing the story of the wealthy family and the way the business and wealth were created can be quite educational for many family members, especially heirs who may not know important details.

For family members to work together successfully, their values, goals, and expectations must be aligned. This alignment helps them truly act as a family rather than simply several people connected by blood and with little else in common. To facilitate the family coherence that enables better decision-making, many families construct vision and mission statements as well as family constitutions.

Your high-performing virtual family office would coordinate the appropriate specialists to help ensure your family works effectively together with the aims that are most important to you. One way to manage the process of family governance is by having family meetings.

Conduct Family Meetings

For many wealthy families, family meetings can help keep the wealthy family together as they result in clarifying the values and concerns that are most important as well as implementing strategies to support family cohesiveness. Many wealthy families also find family meetings to be useful in educating heirs about how to best handle their wealth.

The family meeting principally provides a venue for multiple generations to discuss business and financial issues, as well as relevant personal matters. Common topics include:

- Updates to the succession plans within the family business

- The concerns of family members that impact family enterprises and family relationships

- Promoting business acumen and financial literacy in future generations

- Family philanthropic activities and how they are financially supported

- New business ventures and how to fund them

Family meetings also are times when many wealthy families talk about the values and mission of the family. They also prove to be good opportunities to refine actions taken dealing with family governance.

Your high-performing virtual family office can run impactful family meetings. Very often, an in-house professional with an outside specialist or two is involved in setting up and running family meetings.

Optimizing Family Wealth When Selling a Company

Most private wealth creation, the world over, can be traced back to entrepreneurship. Someone today, or generations past, built a company that has created significant family affluence. Many times, the sale of the company is the source of the family fortune.

Being able to maximize the family's wealth from the sale of their privately held company is usually a major objective (see Chapter 9). That said, based on a plethora of research studies we have conducted over decades, relatively few business owners are doing a very good job of maximizing their family's wealth.

Your high-performing virtual family office would help you prepare your family and your company for sale. This might entail restructuring assets to use trusts to mitigate capital gains to provide investment banking services. It also tends to involve providing wealth management services after the sale, many of which can potentially provide significant tax mitigation benefits.

Corporate Benefits

With privately held businesses the engine of private wealth, being able to deliver corporate benefits is often very important to wealthy families who own companies. There are many different types of corporate benefits with health insurance often being in the highest demand.

Qualified and nonqualified retirement plans are also very attractive to employees. There are a few types of qualified retirement plans, and unfortunately, many wealthy families are not aware of some of them. One type of qualified retirement plan enables the owners to take large tax deductions by putting a substantial amount of money that grows tax deferred (see Chapter 10). The complication is that many professionals are not aware of these types of retirement plans.

Your high-performing virtual family office can evaluate your business situation and show you how different qualified retirement plans would work for you. They will also, if appropriate, show you nonqualified retirement plan possibilities.

Coaching

There are many different versions of coaching. A sizable percentage of wealthy individuals and family members are incredibly motivated to reach higher levels of success. They are looking for direction and guidance in this regard. The answer for a number of them is coaching.

A growing number of coaches concentrate on *personal wealth creation* which is in very high demand by the wealthy. For the most part, these wealth creation authorities are focused on how you need to think (your mindset) and what you need to do (your skillset) to amass greater personal wealth. All personal wealth creation coaches share two important methodologies:

- **Enhancing business relationships:** There is a common focus on strengthening business relationships and finding ways to work more productively with others so that everyone excels.

- **Enhancing business networks:** The ability to leverage and grow business networks is crucial to creating opportunities that translate into greater professional and financial accomplishments.

Whatever form of coaching would significantly benefit family members, your high-performing virtual family office can connect you to the best coaches who can help you achieve your goals. Although these are almost always outside specialists, your high-performing virtual family office provides oversight making sure your objectives and expectations are constantly being met.

Next-Generation Educational Services

Next-generation educational services take many forms and become increasingly fundamental to successfully preparing future wealthy inheritors to manage and lead in today's complex, increasingly transparent, hypercompetitive commercial landscape. Education that is transformative, issues focused, and emphasizes reflective awareness is what future wealthy inheritors are looking for.

The requisite educational approach is geared intently around results. The focus of any viable educational program is to provide an extraordinary and highly actionable curriculum that will enable future wealthy inheritors to excel.

Your high-performing virtual family office can access the specialists that are most appropriate for your situation. Very often, a few experts are engaged to properly address the diverse needs of inheritors.

Because high-performing virtual family offices have an extensive elite team of specialists on call, they can effectively deal with the needs, wants, preferences, and concerns of many wealthy individuals and families. In the next chapter, we will discuss the high-performing virtual family office's elite team.

COMPARING HIGH-PERFORMING SINGLE-FAMILY AND HIGH-PERFORMING VIRTUAL FAMILY OFFICES

In many ways, high-performing virtual family offices aim to duplicate the advantages high-performing single-family offices deliver to the super-rich. Both high-performing single-family offices and high-performing virtual family offices have the same overarching purpose, which is to deliver superior results to wealthy individuals and families.

Here, we will highlight key differences between high-performing single-family offices and high-performing virtual family offices (Exhibit 2.1). Keep in mind that both types of high-performing family offices aim to deliver superior results.

Exhibit 2.1: Comparing Family Offices

CHARACTERISTICS	HIGH-PERFORMING SINGLE-FAMILY OFFICE	HIGH-PERFORMING VIRTUAL FAMILY OFFICE
Business model	Family first	Commercial enterprise
Control	Extensive	Limited
Responsiveness	Complete	High
Use of external experts	Variable but increasingly extensive	Certain experts are in-house and extensive use of outside specialists

Business Model

The mantra of high-performing single-family offices is "Family first." They are bespoke operations designed to address the needs, wants, concerns, and preferences of one super-rich family. On the other hand, high-performing virtual family offices are commercial enterprises. A successful high-performing virtual family office makes money for its owners and employees. In one way or another, high-performing virtual family offices are compensated for the expertise they provide, whether that expertise is in-house or when specialists are brought in.

High-performing single-family offices will provide services and products to family members while taking a financial loss by doing so. Such services are accommodations for family members. This is not the case for high-performing virtual family offices. If your virtual family office is not profitable, it will not be in business for very long.

Control

A major reason the super-rich set up single-family offices is so they have as much control as possible. High-performing single-family offices are truly customized, delivering expertise at the highest levels. The super-rich family is in charge and will get, pretty much, just what it wants.

At high-performing virtual family offices, in contrast, control by any wealthy individual or family is limited. The high-performing virtual family offices will take extensive steps to accommodate the wealthy, but the firm has many wealthy clients and there are protocols to follow.

Responsiveness

High-performing single-family offices are off-the-charts responsive to the needs, wants, concerns, and preferences of their super-rich families. Having quality personnel immediately address concerns—oftentimes irrespective of how frivolous those concerns—is a hallmark of many high-performing single-family offices.

Meanwhile, high-performing virtual family offices are extremely responsive, but there are common limitations because of their business model. Because they need to be responsive to a number of wealthy families, the professionals at high-performing virtual family offices have to manage their time and will likely only drop everything to help a client when the situation is very serious.

Use of External Experts

All types of high-performing family offices tend to make extensive use of external experts. In the case of high-performing single-family offices, the use of external experts is growing because their mandates are expanding. As the super-rich are looking to their high-performing single-family offices to maximize their financial and personal lives, and this means more and more, the need for external experts grows.

At the same time, high-performing virtual family offices are built around bringing in top-quality specialists as needed. This enables them to deliver superior results while managing costs. Specialists maximize the financial and personal lives of a diverse cohort of wealthy clients.

CONCLUSION

Just as there are different types of single-family offices, there are different types of multifamily offices. And going forward, there are likely to be new variations of family offices as the level of private wealth continues to significantly grow worldwide, as technology advances create more opportunities and as clever professionals find innovative ways to deliver exceptional value to an ever-broader array of wealthy individuals and families.

Even though the purpose of high-performing single-family and high-performing virtual family offices is the same—superior results—their business models make them different in very significant ways. Critical is that high-performing single-family offices are all about the family and they are often willing to cover the costs of service provided the super-rich family gets their desired outcomes.

High-performing virtual family offices are commercial enterprises. Although high-performing virtual family offices are also focused on delivering superior results, they are in business to make money—or they will not be around for very long.

We have been talking about high-performing single-family offices and high-performing virtual family offices. We said that a high-performing family office is able to optimize the financial and nonfinancial lives of the wealthy. However, we have not really explained what makes a family office high performing. We will explain this in the next chapter.

3

WHAT MAKES A VIRTUAL FAMILY OFFICE HIGH PERFORMING?

A LOT GOES INTO BUILDING AND GROWING A HIGH-performing virtual family office. For a virtual family office to deliver exceptional value—to be classified as high performing—certain key components are critical.

Consider the following equation:

Integrity + Conviction + Expertise + Process = A High-Performing Virtual Family Office

- **Integrity** is first and foremost. It is an absolute requirement. Without any doubt or hesitancy, the professionals you are working with must always be honorable and upstanding. In this regard, the solutions a high-performing virtual family office provides are amazingly cost effective. However, you need more.

- **Conviction** is the deep desire for the professionals at your high-performing virtual family office to succeed. Keep in mind that they only succeed when you get superior results.

- **Expertise** in the form of services and products is what your high-performing virtual family office provides. In the previous chapter, we talked about the different forms of expertise a high-performing virtual family office is likely to offer. Here, we will discuss your elite team.

- **Process** is how the professional at your high-performing virtual family office interacts with you and other people to deliver superior results.

Always remember that a high-performing virtual family office delivers superior results. This is not possible unless ALL four of these elements are at the highest levels. With integrity given, let us look at the other three components.

CONVICTION

Consider the extremely successful businesspeople you have met. How many of them:

- Are visibly confident in their abilities?

- Radiate a strong sense of purpose?

- Can take command of a situation when necessary?

- Convey the impression they know just what is going on and what needs to be done?

- Are calm and collected, even in tense situations?

- Project a certain type of fearlessness?

These attributes are what you want in your high-performing virtual family office professionals. You want them to convey a sense of purpose and the belief that they can deftly handle situations, even difficult situations.

It is a mental attitude of success that communicates proficiency and supports the idea that they are not only capable but very trustworthy. Breaking it down, conviction embodies dynamism, vitality, and even enthusiasm.

It communicates that they, when appropriate, are in command of the situation. The level of conviction of the professionals at your high-performing virtual family office is critical to delivering exceptional value.

EXPERTISE

We discussed the expertise of many high-performing virtual family offices in the previous chapter. The ability of a high-performing virtual family office to produce superior results is very much dependent on the expertise of the in-house professionals and the capabilities of external experts. Skillfully putting all these talented authorities together and managing the group well results in your elite team.

Exhibit 3.1: Basic Network Structure of the
Virtual Family Office

Your Elite Team

Operationally, one of the biggest differences between the team approach so many professionals proclaim to have and your high-performing virtual family office's elite team is that you are never "handed off" to another professional. You are never referred to anyone else while your high-performing virtual family office professional walks away. When specialists are brought in, the professionals in your high-performing virtual family office always oversee what is going on and make sure you get superior results.

A major advantage of your high-performing virtual family office's elite team is the preferential arrangements available to you (Exhibit 3.2). There are two aspects to preferential arrangements. One is cost mitigation where you either pay less for services and products, or you get more for your money.

Exhibit 3.2: Preferential Arrangements

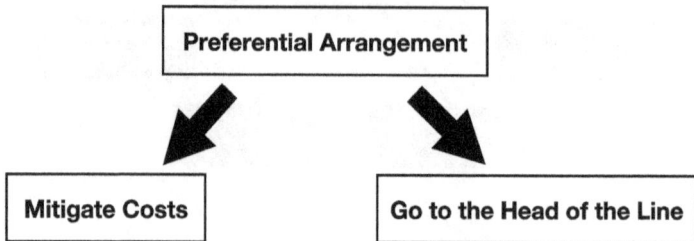

```
        ┌─────────────────────────────┐
        │  Preferential Arrangement   │
        └─────────────────────────────┘
           ↙                      ↘
┌──────────────────┐    ┌─────────────────────────────┐
│  Mitigate Costs  │    │  Go to the Head of the Line │
└──────────────────┘    └─────────────────────────────┘
```

The other aspect of preferential agreements is your ability to jump to the head of the line. Getting access to leading specialists, especially when you want to connect with them, can be difficult. Because these specialists are as good as they are and as renowned as they are, they are in high demand. Nevertheless, because of the expert networks of your high-performing virtual family office professionals, you can regularly move to the very front of the line.

Very importantly, each expert on your high-performing virtual family office's elite team must:

- **Have the highest ethical standards:** Integrity is always essential. All the elite team members have to be scrupulously honest and reliable. There are no excuses for moral lapses of any kind.

- **Be top-of-the-line experts in the field:** What matters is that the members of your high-performing virtual family office's elite team are truly outstanding in their respective fields. It helps majorly if they are also thought leaders, which means they are recognized authorities in their respective fields.

- **Be completely professional:** In every way, such as responsiveness to inquiries and attention to detail, the elite team members embrace professionalism. Another example of professionalism is that the elite team members are continuously learning and even contributing in their area of expertise to stay at the cutting edge of their respective fields.

- **Have personal chemistry with each other:** There should be a strong level of comfort and appreciation among the specialists on your high-performing virtual family office's elite team. When elite team members recognize each other's talents and abilities, their cohesion benefits you all the more extensively.

Your high-performing virtual family office's elite team is filled with leading specialists. Sometimes super-niche specialists are required.

Super-Niche Specialists

Although the specialists required by most of the wealthy (including the super-rich) are easy to source, there are some more elusive super-niche specialists. Even though no services or products are truly unique or 100 percent exclusive in the private wealth industry, some astoundingly talented and experienced professionals are *only* accessible by other professionals who are "in the know." These experts are arguably some of the best at what they do, and what they do is usually extremely specialized, such as:

- A prodigious musical theorist turned world-class professional poker player and Platinum Life Master bridge player (because he decided to spend his time in other pursuits) turned hedging strategist. He is concentrating on developing hedges for passion investments and geopolitical upheavals.

- A one-time juvenile delinquent (the files are sealed) who is currently considered one of the foremost experts on asset protection planning for multijurisdictional successful families. He is credited with helping develop or refine approaches like the "floating island strategy," which works amazingly well but often necessitates that the families are billionaires.

- A Go grandmaster who probably has one of the best track records for winning private trusts and estate lawsuits involving certain offshore jurisdictions. He tends to work for the estates but has been known to play all sides.

While most super-niche specialists deal with wealth management, some address family conflict and family support matters. For example, a former stage magician and mentalist has become an outstandingly accomplished litigation and jury consultant. He is commonly hired when wealthy families engage in civil war.

There are also some exclusive boutique healthcare and family security providers. A reclamation expert—through happenstance—ended up being one of the top professionals when it comes to cult extractions. On the lighter side, there are the cryptozoologist, the cybernetic soothsayer, the quantum matchmaker, and the award-winning dollhouse architect.

Most of the wealthy—including the super-rich—are unlikely to ever require the services of super-niche specialists.

Nevertheless, today, high-performing virtual family offices can access the same super-niche specialists as high-performing single-family offices and it is always nice to know they are available.

PROCESS

Within a high-performing virtual family office, there is integrity, conviction, and expertise. But that is never enough. There must also be a process. All these components are essential. By "process" we are referring to how the professionals at your high-performing virtual family office professionals interact with others—you, your family, and other advisors.

Process is often not seen and many times not even recognized. The more proficient the professionals, the more process becomes a lot like oxygen for the average person. For most people, oxygen is critical to life, invisible, and taken for granted. Most people rarely think about oxygen, but they immediately know when it is not there. Although usually not apparent, process is certainly always "felt."

Like the vast majority of people,

- You probably know when someone truly understands you and when he or she does not.

- You are generally aware if someone you are speaking with is honestly concerned about you or is someone who is just going through the motions.

- You can usually tell when someone truly cares about your well-being and when someone does not.

Process is indisputably critical to making a virtual family office high performing. The professionals at your high-performing virtual family office make a herculean effort to understand you and your world. Only then are they able to deliver exceptional value.

Where so very many professionals seeking to serve wealthy families fail is their inability to uncover the interests of family members. Many professionals presume they know what matters to someone else, and it turns out that a great many times, they are mistaken. Consequently, these professionals are very likely to provide wrong or substandard services and products, thereby producing inferior results. Instead, what characterizes the professionals of your high-performing virtual family office, aside from being quite technically proficient, is that they are adept at determining your goals and concerns. To this end, they depend on a methodology referred to as "discovery" and being empathic.

Discovery

This is how the professionals in your high-performing virtual family office gather information to form meaningful insights that they use to determine the appropriate services and products that will produce superior results.

Through smart questioning, they learn about your world and your interests. When done well, they will understand:

- Your goals and objectives.

- Your critical concerns.

- The way you see yourself and those around you.

- The way your world functions.

Without question, discovery is essential to being able to deliver superior results. Professionals adept at discovery make extensive use of questions to develop a comprehensive picture of you and your world.

You will find your high-performing virtual family office professionals to be intently curious about you, your loved ones, your business interests, and your agenda. Discovery is how they convert that curiosity into action. It is how they ascertain exactly how they can provide you with exceptional value.

Empathy

How the professionals in your high-performing virtual family office make sure they accurately understand you is by being empathetic. Thus, they show concern and ensure that their assessments and interpretations are accurate based on the information they gleaned during discovery.

Empathetic responses confirm whether they are on the right track. Empathy helps reduce errors and misperceptions in all business (and personal) relationships.

You might be dealing with professionals who are technical wizards in their respective fields. However, without the ability to deeply understand you, there is a high probability that the services and products they recommend will be less than optimal.

High-performing virtual family office professionals are quite capable of developing deep, meaningful relationships. They are committed to understanding you and your world. They care about you, which is the cornerstone of being able to deliver superior results.

CONCLUSIONS

There has been an explosion of firms calling themselves virtual family offices, multifamily offices, or claiming to have family office practices. The reality is that a solid percentage of these firms are using the moniker—as we will discuss in the next chapter—because the wealthy are increasingly preferring to work with family offices as opposed to many other types of professionals.

If you are interested in working with a virtual family office, you need to make sure it is high performing. Remember the four essential components to being high performing:

- Integrity

- Conviction

- Expertise

- Process

If the professionals at your virtual family office lack in any of these areas, the probability of getting superior results diminishes greatly.

In the next chapter, we will look at the appeal of high-performing virtual family offices by the wealthy.

4

WHY DO THE WEALTHY INCREASINGLY PREFER VIRTUAL FAMILY OFFICES?

TAKE A MOMENT TO CONSIDER:

If you can have the same advantages as the super-rich, would you *not* want them?

Another question:

If you can have a high-performing single-family office, would you *not* want one?

We find very, very few people saying no to either of these questions. However, the wealthy—for the most part—cannot afford a single-family office. This, however, does not mean they cannot get many of the advantages high-performing single-family offices deliver to the super-rich. For them, the way to get many of those same advantages is by engaging a high-performing virtual family office.

What this means is that the demand for virtual family offices is considerable and growing at an incredible rate. The wealthy, just like the super-rich, want exceptional value. High-performing virtual family offices can maximize the financial world and other aspects of the lives of wealthy individuals and families.

Let us dig a little deeper and consider two ways high-performing virtual family offices steamroll the competition. One way is a disdain for selling. The other way is proficiency in stress testing.

NEVER SELLING

Of critical importance: High-performing virtual family offices **DO NOT SELL** products and services. Instead, they deliver exceptional value in the form of delivering precisely appropriate services and products. This distinction is much more than mere semantics.

To emphasize the point, the difference is not just a difference in terminology. Between these two perspectives, there is a seismic distinction in thinking, approach, and ultimately the level of results achieved (Exhibit 4.1).

Exhibit 4.1: Value versus Selling

FACTORS	DELIVERING VALUE	SELLING
Focus	You	Themselves
Approach	The professional finds meaningful ways to make a significant difference in your life	Persuade you to buy some service or product
Success criteria	Superior results	Sales

When professionals sell, they are *not* focusing on what matters most to you. Instead, they are focused heavily on what matters to them. The fact that your high-performing virtual family office **DOES NOT SELL** proves to be a major boon to you as well as a point of differentiation.

Your high-performing virtual family office is not attempting to persuade you in any way. The professionals at your high-performing virtual family office are not trying to convince you.

By providing services and products that precisely match up to your expressed needs, latent needs, wants, and wishes, your financial and personal life—including the lives of your loved ones as well as the causes you care about—majorly benefit. Your high-performing virtual family office is delivering answers that are most meaningful to you.

The Art of *NOT SELLING*

A truly comprehensive and holistic orientation is one of the most powerful advantages of your high-performing virtual family office. The ability of the professionals to understand the complexities in your life to help you most effectively address your wishes, requirements, concerns, and preferences, enables them to add value in ways that make an enormous difference. The products and services of your high-performing virtual family office are made available when they are precisely appropriate—and only then.

To reiterate: Selling is when people try to convince or persuade you to use their services and products. The professionals in your high-performing virtual family office practice use discovery and are empathic to determine what matters to you so they can deliver exceptional value.

THE POWER OF STRESS TESTING

Stress testing is a very common practice among high-performing single-family offices and high-performing virtual family offices. It is a powerful methodology to better ensure that you are making smart decisions concerning your wealth and key aspects of your personal life. Stress testing is an effective way to find what are usually big problems and make changes to get superior results before it is too late.

Based on research we have conducted with the wealthy over decades, some of them are quite confident as to the actions they are taking and the fact they are considering all viable possible actions. However, only a very small percentage of them feel this way. The numbers run about one in five. The rest of the wealthy are *not* particularly confident. Whether we are talking about actions they have taken or if they are considering all viable possibilities available to them, most of them are not very confident at all.

Usually, the wealthy have a few concerns about the actions they have taken and a few concerns about missing out on other actions that might prove fruitful. When we have these types of conversations with the wealthy about their financial and family lives, most of them grow anxious because they simply do not know where they stand.

To ensure you are getting superior results, your high-performing virtual family office will engage in stress testing.

One way to think about stress testing is,

> **Stress testing is a systematic way to evaluate whether the financial and related services and products you are using will deliver the results you expect and to ensure that you are not missing any meaningful opportunities.**

Put another way,

> **Stress testing is a systematic process for your high-performing virtual family office to rapidly find ways to deliver superior results.**

Stress testing is very effective in:

- Avoiding potentially economically and legally destructive situations.

- Making sure you benefit from all possible opportunities (Exhibit 4.2).

Exhibit 4.2: Stress Testing Objectives

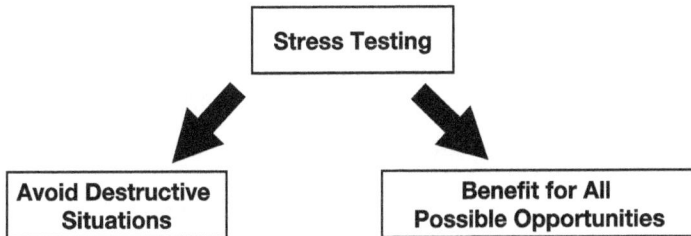

```
                    ┌─────────────────┐
                    │  Stress Testing │
                    └─────────────────┘
              ↙                          ↘
┌──────────────────────┐      ┌──────────────────────────┐
│  Avoid Destructive   │      │      Benefit for All      │
│     Situations       │      │  Possible Opportunities   │
└──────────────────────┘      └──────────────────────────┘
```

When you are dealing with a high-performing virtual family office, stress testing unobtrusively starts with discovery. Through discovery and by being empathetic, the professionals at your high-performing virtual family office determine if some of the actions you have taken might not produce their desired results. If you know what you did was inaccurate or insufficient or, more likely, if you are unsure and this is an issue, then the stress testing process moves forward.

The Stress Testing Process

The following are the three steps to stress testing (Exhibit 4.3).

Exhibit 4.3: The Stress Testing Process

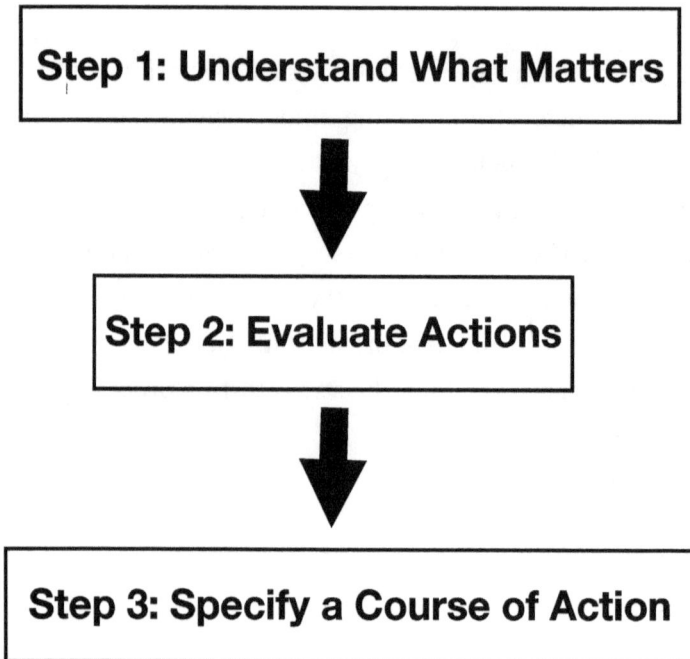

```
┌─────────────────────────────────────────┐
│   Step 1: Understand What Matters        │
└─────────────────────────────────────────┘
                    ↓
       ┌──────────────────────────────┐
       │   Step 2: Evaluate Actions   │
       └──────────────────────────────┘
                    ↓
┌─────────────────────────────────────────┐
│  Step 3: Specify a Course of Action     │
└─────────────────────────────────────────┘
```

- **Step 1: The professionals at your high-performing virtual family office understand what matters to you and what does not.** Through discovery and by being empathetic, they will understand what you require and your desired outcomes. At this point, it is not about how to get where you want to go; it is about where you want to go.

- **Step 2: Evaluate the actions that have been taken and actions that are being considered.** Once your high-performing virtual family office professionals fully understand your goals and concerns, they need to have at hand all the relevant documentation on the services and products they will evaluate. The assumptions behind each service or product will be systematically altered to determine how the current and proposed solutions will work when the what-ifs of the scenarios change. Also, the cost structure will be analyzed to see if a more cost-effective alternative makes sense.

- **Step 3: Specify a course of action.** Based on the evaluation of the existing or proposed services and products, the professionals at your high-performing virtual family office will recommend a course of action (Exhibit 4.4).

Exhibit 4.4: Courses of Action after Stress Testing

COURSE OF ACTION	CRITICAL FACTORS
Stay the course	The current services or products are appropriate
Choose different solutions	A system fail
Choose a different professional	The services or products are appropriate, but the professionals involved are not truly capable and/or are cost inefficient
Modified approach with original professional	A little tweaking is required
Continue stress testing or get another opinion	Have a different professional conduct the evaluation or provide a third opinion

To get an idea of how stress testing works, let us consider some examples of stress testing with the super-rich.

EXAMPLES OF STRESS TESTING WITH THE SUPER-RICH

Stress testing can be all-inclusive, where you look at everything going on in a super-rich family. Most times, stress testing focuses on a particular issue or set of circumstances or something a super-rich family member has done, such as their estate planning or the way they have structured their business projects. The following are four examples of stress testing with the super-rich.

Example 1: Customized Premium Financed Life Insurance

A billionaire family purchased life insurance for several family members to address succession issues and to potentially generate significant investment returns. The solution was a highly customized multilayered premium life insurance transaction delivering many, many hundreds of millions of dollars in death benefits at an astoundingly low cost accompanied by completely tax-free investment returns.

Involved in the transaction were:

- An international life insurance specialist

- A cadre of lawyers

- An offshore reinsurance company

- One boutique investment bank

- A family office consortium in conjunction with a very substantial investment fund provided the loans to pay the premiums

The transaction is exceedingly complicated and it made some of the family members nervous. Overall, they clearly understood there was potential for things to go wrong and were, therefore, concerned about the risks. They wanted to be certain they knew all the risks, which led them to question the transaction.

A leading international tax lawyer referred us to senior management at the family's single-family office. After being retained and getting an overview of the transaction, we assembled a team of specialists mirroring the group involved who executed the transaction. One of the experts we brought in is off the grid and was only available because of our previous business dealings. It took the team a couple of months to critically evaluate the transaction.

Bottom line: The transaction effectively addresses the needs and wants of the super-rich family. It is also 100 percent legitimate. Moreover, the professionals that put the transaction together were quite clever about it. The family members were very happy knowing that the actions they took were verified and confirmed.

Example 2: Fair Does Not Mean "Right"

An evaluation of the estate plan of an extremely wealthy business owner pinpointed the differences in the family dynamics between the time the estate plan was originally signed and today. The likely outcome after his death would have been an all-out war among his four adult children. The family conflict would also likely have been the death knell for the more than 200-year-old family business.

In determining inheritances, the patriarch had gone with "even" instead of "fair" on the advice of counsel. Each child would have received an equal share of the estate, including the company, even though only one of the four was involved in the company—as president. The patriarch described two of the children as "do-nothings" and "worthless" and a lot of other things we cannot put to paper.

Bottom line: Thinking through the situation with an intense focus on the founder's self-interest resulted in a new estate plan and a well-structured business succession plan which was also a rigorous asset protection plan. The child in the company will get sole ownership and control of the company. The other children will get comparable amounts of wealth but in different forms that they cannot easily decimate.

Example 3: Illegal Tax Planning

A super-rich entrepreneur was actually quite proud of how ingenious his tax planning was and how well it worked. The complication was that some of his business dealings were being scrutinized and he wanted to make absolutely sure his tax planning would not cause him any problems. His tax plan had done a number of things:

- He transferred some of his businesses to a trust for which he received units of beneficial interest. The business trust makes payments to him, thereby avoiding taxes. The business trust will also not have to pay future estate taxes.

- In another jurisdiction, he sold appreciated property to another trust in exchange for an annuity, which in turn sold the assets and reinvested the money. He claims recognition of the built-in gain over his life, and the trust is not included in the estate.

- He transferred his family home to yet another trust and received units that were claimed to be part of a taxable exchange, resulting in a stepped-up basis for the property. The trust is thus in the rental business and claims to rent the residence back to him. He does not pay rent because he is the caretaker of the property.

- He created a hierarchy of trusts owning other trusts. One trust on top, in effect, holds the trust units of a total of forty-one trusts and this trust distributes the income from those trusts.

It became clear very quickly that he and his advisors had created many trusts, some dubious in nature, that held selected assets and income streams. A big criminal mistake was that by vertically layering many of these trusts, arguably fraudulent expenses were being charged to subsequent trusts, resulting in a decrease in taxable income. Simultaneously, the approach resulted in the illusion of separation of control to protect the assets in the trusts.

Creating abusive trusts and layering them the way he did can come in a wide variety of forms, with almost all of them being used for questionable, if not illegal, purposes. It is analogous to Russian matryoshka dolls where one doll is hidden within a similar doll. Unless all the dolls are opened, you cannot find the only one that is not hollow.

Bottom line: In this case, the super-rich entrepreneur claimed he thought he was just being smart about his tax planning. What he was doing in places was illegal, and even if he did not know it, the advisors who guided him and did the work most assuredly did. Irrespective, he was on the hook for this planning. He completely redid all his wealth planning.

Example 4: Too Much Money Too Soon

We reviewed a will where the youngest son, currently six years of age, would, on turning twelve, receive an inheritance of slightly more than $250 million. Who would hand this much money over to a twelve-year-old? Not many super-rich families would hand over a quarter of a billion dollars to a twelve-year-old and this family would *not* think of doing so.

The technical failure was the transposition of two numbers. The will was supposed to read that the son inherits the fortune at twenty-one years of age, not twelve. However, who would hand this much money over to a twenty-one-year-old? How many super-rich families would entrust $250 million to a twenty-one-year-old when that person is only six years old today? We pointed out that it might be "safer" to give a twelve-year-old $250 million than give a twenty-one-year-old that amount.

Some extremely wealthy families might hand a quarter of a billion dollars to a twenty-one-year-old without restriction, but this family was appalled by the idea. There was a serious breakdown in communication between the super-rich family and the advisors involved in putting together the estate plan.

Bottom line: The super-rich family's estate plan was dramatically adjusted and updated. At the moment, it is currently tightly aligned with the super-rich family's overall agenda, and the son will inherit substantial wealth in a very disciplined manner, but not a quarter of a billion dollars when he turns twelve or twenty-one. The estate plan delivers the framework and structure for creating a family dynasty while better insulating family members from losing wealth through taxes, litigation, or divorce.

COMPARING STRESS TESTING FOR THE SUPER-RICH AND THE WEALTHY

Stress testing, as we discussed, is quite common for the super-rich. A large percentage of high-performing single-family offices are regularly engaged in stress testing to make sure the super-rich are achieving optimal outcomes. Meanwhile, stress testing is becoming more and more prevalent among the wealthy who are far from being super-rich, in large part because of high-performing virtual family offices. Making sure mistakes are not made and that wealthy families are not missing out is something they all tend to want.

Based on our research and extensive experience, there is at present a poignant difference between stress testing with the super-rich and stress testing with the wealthy. Generally speaking, stress testing by the super-rich tends to find fewer errors or opportunities for improvement compared to those less wealthy. This is probably due to the caliber of professionals engaged by many super-rich families and their high-performing single-family offices. Their approach to due diligence can be quite intense. However, when "failings" are found, they tend to be quite severe.

More Mistakes among the Less Wealthy

Generally, stress testing for the wealthy turns up issues that range from mildly problematic, where some minor refinements get the desired results, to much more severe problems where the intended goals are not being achieved and the outcomes can even be very detrimental. It is also common to find significantly more errors and missed opportunities.

Stress testing, for instance, can often uncover deadly "back doors" to a wealthy individual's or a family's asset protection plans. For example, some extremely successful entrepreneurs place different companies in separate entities. This helps protect the different companies if something bad happens to one of them. However, such an approach fails to insulate those entities from adversities that may occur in the personal lives of wealthy entrepreneurs. This failure is quite prevalent among a great many business owners and real estate entrepreneurs. However, when it comes to the super-rich, the back doors are usually locked tight.

It happens quite often that wealthy individuals and families purchase life insurance that is inappropriate for their needs. They may buy too much life insurance or the life insurance is not structured properly. Keep in mind that before purchasing life insurance to pay estate taxes, you want to take every legal step to mitigate these taxes. This, unfortunately, is not always the case. Stress testing will ensure that the right amount of life insurance is purchased and that it is set up properly.

Another example where stress testing is regularly useful for successful entrepreneurs is evaluating their qualified retirement plans. A large percentage of accomplished entrepreneurs can take larger income tax deductions by using sophisticated defined benefit plans, but they and the advisors they are relying on are unaware of these possibilities. Because of stress testing, potentially missed opportunities are discovered.

Again, why is stress testing likely to uncover more problems among the wealthy than the super-rich? The principal reason appears to be the level of capabilities of the professionals initially engaged and the limited amount of oversight of these professionals.

Many of the wealthy are probably dealing with professionals who, while they intend on doing a good job, lack the expertise and ability to deliver solid, let alone superior, results. What makes the situation more complicated is that these professionals do not even know what they don't know and that they are, indeed, quite technically limited.

The issue is not the intent or even integrity of the professionals but their bounded sophistication and proficiencies. At the same time, the super-rich often, through their high-performing single-family offices, are very attuned to what the professionals they engage are doing. High-performing single-family offices closely monitor their external experts.

Stress testing is a powerful advantage the super-rich have because of their high-performing single-family offices. It is an advantage you can also have when you engage a high-performing virtual family office. The professional in your high-performing virtual family office can be instrumental in making sure you are not making any serious mistakes or missing any meaningful opportunities.

CONCLUSION

The incredible growth in private wealth the world over appears to only be superseded by the number of professionals seeking to do business with the wealthy. Although there are a plethora of professionals seeking to serve the wealthy, many, many of them are not up to the job. Nevertheless, these less-than-adept professionals are not going to let a lack of knowledge or skill slow them down.

The way many professionals seek to gain a strong marketing edge is to refer to their firms as virtual family offices. It does not matter if these professionals can deliver superior results. What often matters more to so many of them is closing the wealthy prospect.

Why is there a substantial marketing advantage for professionals to say they have a virtual family office?

The answer is quite simple:

The wealthy want many of the same advantages high-performing single-family offices provide their super-rich families and this is possible when they engage high-performing virtual family offices.

PART II

SELECTED EXPERTISE

THERE IS NOTHING UNIQUE IN THE WORLD OF FAMILY offices. If your virtual family office is high performing, it can deliver all the expertise you require to help you optimize your financial and personal lives. At the same time, other high-performing virtual family offices can deliver the same expertise.

The complication is that most self-professed virtual family offices or multifamily offices or family office practices are NOT high performing. So many professionals and firms have latched on to some variation of the term "family office" because the wealthy are regularly choosing some form of family office over other types of providers such as private banks, law firms, wealth management firms, and accounting firms.

Although we say that your virtual family office is not offering unique products and services, many times they de facto are. That is, they are able to provide powerful solutions that many in the private wealth industry are unfamiliar with or are not capable of effectively implementing.

In Part II, we will talk about some basic and some sophisticated services and products available from a high-performing virtual family office. The VFO Advisory Group provides the complete range of expertise, including what we discuss in Part II, to our clients.

5

WHAT IS AN ESTATE PLAN?

BY J. ALAN SOELBERG AND VINCE ANNABLE

Estate planning is essential to most wealthy individuals and families. It is the way to ensure that the wishes and agenda of the wealthy are fulfilled when they pass away. As such, estate planning is a common need and is, therefore, a critical service of a high-performing virtual family office.

What is going to happen to the wealth you have accumulated should you have the bad judgment to pass away?

High-net-worth individuals and families who may be very sophisticated at business are often surprisingly unsophisticated about even the basics of estate planning. An even larger number continually put off making plans for their estate, sometimes until it is too late. Making and executing a plan takes time and effort, but it is time and effort well spent.

Let us not fool ourselves by pretending that it is easy or pleasant to think about, much less plan for, your inevitable demise. However, as with the sale of a business, it is always better to start planning earlier than later. Remember the old saying that Benjamin Franklin is believed to have first come up with in 1789:

In this world, nothing can be said to be certain, except death and taxes.

DRAWING UP YOUR WILL

You want to determine what will happen to your assets after your death. If you do not take steps to do this, not you but the laws of your state will make those determinations. This is what you want to avoid by planning ahead.

The first step in estate planning is drawing up a will. If you die intestate—that is, without having formulated a will—a court will determine who is entitled to inherit your assets and how. This is what you want, above all, to avoid.

Let's take a simple example. Say you own a Rolex watch and a Timex. Who gets the Rolex? Who gets the Timex? Who gets neither? More generally, who is entitled to what part of your assets, and who is not entitled to anything?

Also, it is critical to be aware of and account for the fact that a will only applies to assets in your own name. If you and a business partner have a joint checking account, on your death the assets in the account will revert to your surviving business partner, not to your own estate.

ESTABLISHING A TRUST

Your will, if you have one, will be probated once you have the bad judgment to die. The dictionary definition of probate is "the official proving of a will." In other words, even if you have written a will, it needs to be legally validated, and this is generally done in a probate court.

In this case, the court decides not how your assets should be distributed according to the laws of your state but whether the instructions you have set forth in your will are legally valid. This is generally the case, but it is also possible for the heir who got the Timex watch rather than the Rolex to contest the terms of your will.

Not only do you not want to die intestate, but you want to

avoid probate as much as you can. The best way to do this is to establish trust. Trusts come in many different varieties. For example, we have already looked at the deferred sales trust. Trusts are basically legal entities to which you can transfer your assets. Once this is done, the trust, rather than you as an individual, now owns and controls these assets. This transfer of ownership can have many legal, tax, and other benefits.

In the case of wealth transfer, you want to establish a living trust, which is a trust that continues to "live" after you die. If this trust owns your business, house, or other real estate and investment assets, it retains ownership of those assets even after you die.

In establishing the trust, you have the authority to incorporate directives as to how the trust should deal with those assets. To avoid confusion, understand that a will cannot own anything and controls only assets held in an individual's name at death. A trust is a legal entity capable of owning assets. Essentially, your directives incorporate the instructions in your will into the trust. They turn your will into an integral part of the living trust.

These directives specify how you want your assets to be handled. Say the trust is drawn up while you still own your business. Should you die before the business is sold or otherwise transferred, your directives can state exactly what you want to be done with the business. For example, you can specify who should take it over and run it. How much ownership should so-and-so have? Should someone who might have inherited the business if you had died intestate receive no ownership position at all?

The same is true of your real estate, investments, and other assets—not only who gets the Rolex and who gets the Timex but who gets the house. If you have several children, should one of them inherit your primary residence? Or should it be sold, and all your children receive an equal share of the profits?

Many directives in a trust are standard legal "boilerplate," meaning they are the same in most or almost all such trusts. However, there are always specific, individual circumstances. Say that you have children who are still minors. Should they be entitled to an inheritance immediately after your death or only after turning twenty-one? Do you feel, for whatever reason, that they would be better served if they waited until a while longer, say until age thirty, to come into their inheritance?

In the final analysis, a trust is a particularly effective tool for protecting your assets for your beneficiaries, such as your children. It is they, as your beneficiaries, who will benefit the most from the trust.

DESIGNATING A TRUSTEE

A trust essentially allows you to retain control of your assets from beyond the grave. You and your spouse will generally be the executors of a living trust while you are still alive. You should also designate a successor trustee to take over the administration of the trust upon your death.

Whomever you appoint as trustee should, quite literally, be someone you can trust. The trustee should be someone whose judgment and honesty you rely on and who is willing to follow the directives you have set out in the trust. A trustee does not have to be a financial or legal expert because they can hire lawyers, accountants, and investment advisors to give them expert assistance when necessary.

MEDICAL DIRECTIVES

Before we get into the ways of using trusts to legally protect your assets from taxes and other liabilities, let us return to you personally. Since it is likely that you will be ill before you pass away, it is critical that your trust contain a medical directive as well as financial ones.

The cornerstone of a healthcare directive is conferring medical power of attorney on someone you trust to make medical decisions for you. To clarify, power of attorney permits someone else to act on your behalf and in your interests while you are still alive. The individual given your medical power of attorney may or may not be the person you have designated as trustee of your living trust.

Your health may be such that while you are still alive, you become incapacitated and therefore unable to make decisions about medical care for yourself. Granting medical power of attorney to, for example, one of your children gives them the authority to make these decisions for you.

Your medical directive can place restrictions on these decisions.

You can specify how long you want to be on a life support system, such as a ventilator, if you are in a terminal condition or persistent vegetative state. Do you wish to remain in this state for as long as possible or only for so long and no longer? You can also specify whether or not you want to be resuscitated if you go into a coma. You may wish to specify whether you want to become an organ donor upon your demise. On the other hand, you might prefer to leave one or more of these decisions entirely up to the person with your medical power of attorney, trusting them to act in your best interests when you're no longer capable of making decisions for yourself.

IRREVOCABLE TRUSTS AND
TAX MITIGATION

The terms of a living trust can be changed, amended, or revoked up to the time of your death. An irrevocable trust, on the other hand, is a trust where assets you have deposited cannot be retrieved during your lifetime, nor has its terms changed, at least not easily. To simplify a complex legal matter: one reason to establish an irrevocable trust is to mitigate the taxes your heirs might otherwise be required to pay on your assets after you pass away.

Let us take one tax mitigation strategy as an example. Say your estate is worth $10 million. The concern is that your heirs will have to pay several million of those dollars in taxes when you die.

One solution to this problem is to create an irrevocable trust into which you place $100,000 or more. The trust, not you as an individual, can then buy a life insurance policy naming you as the insured. Premiums on the policy will be paid as necessary from the funds in the trust. Although you are the insured, the irrevocable life insurance trust is the policy owner since you no longer have any control over the assets in the trust. Then, when you have the bad judgment to die, the life insurance benefits are paid into the trust.

Your heirs will then become the beneficiaries of the life

insurance policy the trust owns. Since the trust owns the policy and not you, these life insurance benefits are not included as part of your estate. The end result is that your heirs are now entitled to receive those benefits tax-free.

To put the matter in round figures, say your estate is $10 million and the benefits from your life insurance policy are another $10 million. When you die, your estate will be worth $10 million, rather than $20 million, since the $10 million in benefits is controlled by an irrevocable trust, which paid the premiums on the policy while you were still alive. The benefits of the policy then go directly to its beneficiaries, who will also most probably be the heirs of your estate.

INSTALLMENT TRUSTS

A second example where an irrevocable trust might provide some significant tax assistance comes in the form of what is commonly referred to as an "installment trust" (Exhibit 5.1). One of the greatest concerns of any "seller" of equity is the consequential income and capital gains tax treatment.

An installment trust can address these issues by strategically selling a portion of the equity in the seller's entity to an irrevocable trust prior to the sale to the cash buyer. In this transaction between seller and trust, rather than paying cash to the seller, the trust finances the purchase of the equity in the seller's entity with a promissory note wherein the trust is the "maker" who owes the money, and the seller is the "holder" who is owed the money.

In other words, this third-party trust first purchases a portion of the asset and pays the seller back over time. When the subsequent sale to the cash buyer is effectuated, cash is allocated to the trust proportionate to the trust's equity ownership in the seller, and that cash is invested, with that principal and interest held in the trust used to pay the seller pursuant to the terms of the promissory note between seller and trust.

In order to address the concerns, the trust must be a true third party, and the transaction between the seller and trust must be an arm's-length transaction, at fair market value. A third-party fiduciary serves as the grantor and trustee of this trust.

The beneficiaries of the trust cannot be the seller or seller's principals where the seller is an entity, otherwise it is not a true third-party, arm's-length transaction. However, in certain circumstances where planning is implemented far enough in advance, the beneficiaries can be selected by the seller.

As previously mentioned, the sale between the seller and the trust is structured as an installment sales contract.

Payment terms on the promissory note can be set in advance. With those payments now subject to the time frame outlined in the term of the promissory note, tax consequences are spread out over a period of time, allowing the seller to defer tax payment while generating income due to the interest rate associated with the promissory note.

These are just two examples of many different types of trusts and trust strategies that exist and have specific tax and other advantages.

Exhibit 5.1: Irrevocable Installment Trust

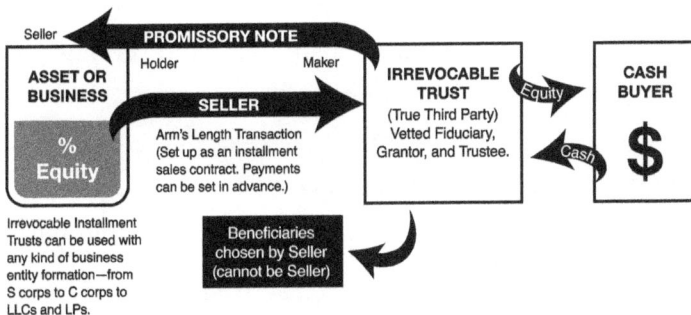

LAST WORDS

A living trust is just that: a living document. It cannot just be drawn up and set aside. It needs to be reviewed and updated from time to time. Say you draw up the trust, as you should, while you still own a business. The trust will need to be revised when and if the business is sold. Say your oldest child is still in elementary school when the trust is first drawn. Once your youngest child turns twenty-one, the directives in the trust will undoubtedly need to be revised.

The truth, however unfortunate, is that Benjamin Franklin, as usual, was right about death and taxes. At some point, you and your spouse will have the bad judgment to pass away. What then happens can remain largely in your control but only if you take concerted and realistic action.

Such action can also be taken to protect your assets from lawsuits and other potential liabilities. Not everyone you come into contact with is going to be scrupulous.

The key message is to make sure that you have put your financial house in order by establishing a living trust and, if appropriate, an irrevocable trust.

6

WHAT ARE BENEFIT-FOCUSED RETIREMENT PLANS?

BY FRANK V. SENECO AND ROBERT ANNABLE

THERE ARE SEVERAL DIFFERENT TYPES OF QUALI-fied retirement plans available to successful entrepreneurs. The complication is that a great many professionals are not familiar with some of the more sophisticated qualified retirement plans such as the benefit-focused retirement plan. High-performing virtual family offices can capably provide the best-qualified retirement plan to each successful entrepreneur. Here's an example to show how it works.

Robert and Susan Marks own a very successful consulting company that they started ten years ago in California. Robert (age fifty-nine) and Susan (age fifty-seven) have done well since starting the business, revenues have grown over the years, and now they are seeing profits in excess of $2.5 million. They have also brought their three adult children into the business and intend to have them take over within ten years.

Being California residents, the couple is subject to a combined income tax rate of 50 percent. Looking for ways to legitimately reduce their tax burden and knowing they want to retire and transfer the business to the children, their accountant suggested they look at establishing a retirement plan.

With the couple looking to make large pretax contributions into a retirement plan for themselves and their children who are employees, the CPA suggested a defined benefit pension plan.

They reviewed multiple proposals, and with a traditional defined benefit plan, the maximum pretax contribution they were projected to make was approximately $450,000. This calculation includes what is referred to as a cash balance plan, which lets people make larger contributions than many traditional defined benefit plans. Although not a bad result, Robert and Susan asked if there was a way to contribute more for themselves and their children, thereby lowering their income tax bill even more.

The accountant then suggested they consider a benefit-focused plan that provides multiple benefits to the plan participants—the couple and their children. With a benefit-focused retirement plan, the Markses are able to fund a pretax contribution of $1,425,000 in year one and can contribute in excess of $1.2 million per year over the next five years.

The plan would provide Robert and Susan with a combined $40,000 per month in retirement income. They would each receive $20,000 per month of joint and survivor lifetime income when they retire as well as accrue pension benefits for their children.

QUALIFIED RETIREMENT PLANS

A qualified retirement plan is a retirement plan sanctioned by the IRS. The contributions made to the plan are almost always income tax deductible. The monies in the plan grow tax-deferred. It is not until the plan participant takes the money out that the income is taxed. The logic is that when participants take money out of their qualified retirement plan, there is a lot more money because the funds are compounded at a greater rate because of a lack of taxes. Also, for many participants, when they do take their money, they are in a lower tax bracket.

There are two main types of qualified retirement plans.

One type is a defined contribution plan. The most common of these plans are 401(k) plans and employer-sponsored profit-sharing plans. In general, defined contribution plans have limits on the amounts that can be contributed to them. With defined contribution plans, the employees will contribute to the 401(k) plan and the company will—many times—match a portion of their contribution.

The other type of qualified retirement plan is a defined benefit plan. These are employer-sponsored retirement plans. The amount that can be contributed for each employee is based on actuarial formulas that take into account various factors such as age, length of employment, and salary.

With defined benefit plans, because they are based on actuarial formulas, often entrepreneurs can contribute much larger pretax contributions to fund retirement benefits. With a traditional defined benefit plan, a participant receives a monthly income for their individual lifetime starting at retirement. The maximum monthly retirement that can be provided for 2022 is $20,416.67 or $245,000 annually. The monthly retirement benefit is indexed for inflation typically on an annual basis, so it increases each year. As with a defined contribution plan, the assets in a defined benefit plan grow tax deferred and are taxable when they are received by the participant.

BENEFIT-FOCUSED PLANS

The benefit-focused plan is a defined benefit pension plan. It is a more sophisticated retirement plan that can provide greater benefits than traditional defined benefit plans and tends to work especially well for successful entrepreneurs running smaller businesses based on the number of employees. It also works very well for celebrities and high-income earners.

What is important to realize is that benefit-focused plans are not that common because many wealth managers, accountants, and attorneys are not familiar with them. This results in a substantial percentage of entrepreneurs missing out.

Using established pension benefit design opportunities that are clearly codified, the benefit-focused plan provides business owners, for example, with the ability to build a retirement plan that can provide a lifetime of benefits for themselves, their surviving spouses, and family members. The benefit-focused plan is not new, as the concept of providing lifetime benefits for plan participants and spouses has existed for decades. However, the Pension Protection Act of 2006 solidified opportunities that have been used for many years by large corporations.

The benefit-focused plan is sophisticated. It can provide the business owner with a qualified retirement plan that:

- Develops financial resources that cannot be outlived

- Keeps pace with inflation and grows income tax-free

- Is protected from the claims of creditors

- Potentially is not subject to federal estate or state inheritance taxes

- Reserves for all life's contingencies from living too long, dying too soon, becoming disabled, or needing long-term medical assistance

Furthermore, the benefit-focused plan benefits can include:

- Lifetime retirement benefits for the participant and surviving spouse

- A death benefit pre-retirement

- A post-retirement with IRS approval

- Disability benefits equal to the projected retirement benefit

- Post-retirement medical reimbursement with long-term care benefits

By combining all these benefits together in the plan design, many entrepreneurs, for instance, can provide the highest tax-deductible contributions possible. This allows them to have their monies increase faster while being creditor protected.

The following are examples of some additional case examples where benefit-focused plans proved advantageous:

- Two business owners ages sixty-three and fifty-two have a distribution company with twenty-two employees. One of the owners intends to retire in approximately seven years while the other one will stay and run the company. The business owners are able to put $1,881,296 in year one into the plan with additional annual payments actuarially calculated. About 87 percent of the benefits from the plan will go to the business owners.

- Two business owners ages fifty and fifty-one with no employees are looking for large pension contributions to ensure a lifetime pension income. They are able to put away $1,019,122 in year one with additional annual payments actuarially calculated. Because the staff for their office is covered by the hospital, they receive 100 percent of the benefits.

· Three dentists ages fifty-eight, fifty-eight, and fifty-one own and run a successful practice with eight employees. They are able to put $2,019,157 in year one into the plan with additional annual payments actuarially calculated. About 97 percent of the money will go to the three dentists.

It is important for entrepreneurs, professionals, and their advisors to recognize that although benefit-focused plans are often great ways to lower income taxes while creating a large pool of retirement assets, they are not one-and-done. So that they stay in compliance, these plans must be reviewed annually or when major changes occur like an acquisition. To continue to get the benefits, these plans might need to be tweaked as circumstances change.

CONCLUSION

There are powerful advantages to qualified retirement plans. To be more precise, qualified retirement plans are legitimate tax shelters. The federal government is providing these tax advantages to help motivate people to save for retirement.

What is valuable is for entrepreneurs, celebrities, and high-income earners interested in paying less income taxes and saving for retirement to consider all the possible retirement plans available to them. This includes the benefit-focused plan. Unfortunately, because the benefit-focused plan is complicated compared to other qualified retirement plans, many professionals are not aware of it.

By comparing ALL the different qualified retirement plans, many entrepreneurs, celebrities, and high-income earners choose the benefit-focused plan because of the multitude of benefits they can receive. It is something to certainly consider.

7

WHAT IS WEALTH ENHANCEMENT?

BY VINCE ANNABLE

A CAPABILITY OF HIGH-PERFORMING VIRTUAL FAMILY offices that is not common among many other types of professionals is a focus on wealth enhancement. The ability to legitimately lessen the tax burden is a powerful way to ensure wealth is maintained. Wealth enhancement is the cornerstone of high-performing virtual family offices.

One client was referred to us in October 2020 to assist them in mitigating their taxes. They were experiencing an explosion in their business and thus creating a very large future tax bill. Because we were able to start their tax planning in the same year they were experiencing this significant increase in income, we were able to implement before-year-end tax mitigation strategies that took their projected tax bill of over $900,000 to a much more manageable $130,000. We were able to implement strategies that eliminated, deferred, and prepared them for their tax obligation for the tax year 2020.

A significant percentage of affluent families are NOT maximizing their wealth in this way. An effective approach to enhancing wealth is to mitigate the amount you pay in taxes. The aim is to save as much of your hard-earned cash for yourself as you legally can. The more you save in taxes, the more you have to invest for your future.

Tax planning is regularly the key to wealth enhancement. The problem is that tax and cash-flow planning often take a back seat or are confused with tax preparation. The two, though related, are very different.

TAX PLANNING COMPARED TO TAX PREPARATION

The VFO Advisory Group team includes CPAs whose focus is wider than you generally encounter. Many CPAs work in areas unconnected to taxes, but probably eight or nine out of ten CPAs who do work in taxes concern themselves almost entirely with tax preparation and compliance. Although tax preparation and compliance are important, tax planning before the final preparation of tax returns is even more so if you want to enhance your wealth.

The question you should ask yourself is this: Does your current CPA, accountant, or tax preparer only do tax preparation—that is, your tax returns—or do they also get involved in providing tax-planning strategies that reduce your taxes? For a significant number of CPAs, their response is probably "only tax preparation." There's much more to tax planning than giving your preparer or accountant your records and receipts in a shoebox and getting back your return to sign and send to the IRS along with a check.

It makes a lot more sense to prepare for tax day by reducing the size of the check you must write. Most accountants spend most of their time looking in the rearview mirror and almost none are looking at how to reduce client tax liability. This is a retrospective rather than a prospective process. Tax planning means looking ahead through the windshield as well as the rearview mirror. Tax planning is proactive and tax preparation is reactive. Once the end of the year rolls around, it's too late to start planning.

Accountancy and mastery of tax laws are highly specialized fields that often involve decades of experience. It would be impossible to cover the entire gamut of tax-planning strategies even in several books entirely devoted to the subject. What we'll do here is lay out some general principles illustrated with specific strategies. Think of these as tools in a larger toolbox.

Many high-net-worth individuals are business owners, and certain tax-planning strategies specifically apply to owned-and-operated businesses. More generally, it's critical to realize that tax planning comes in three varieties: current-year tax planning, next-year tax planning, and long-term tax planning. You'll find an example of long-term planning later in the chapter. Let's focus on the shorter terms first.

ELIMINATE AND DEFER

Tax planning involves what-if scenarios:

- What happens if we do such and such?

- What happens to our tax situation if we make this investment?

- What happens to our tax situation if we make that other investment?

Tax planning is all about laying out plausible scenarios, determining in advance what can be done to help you plan for, and wherever legally possible, mitigate your taxes. These scenarios fall into three categories: eliminating, deferring, and paying your taxes.

The first thing tax planning does is eliminate taxes wherever legally possible. The second is to defer taxes from this to next year or some other future time. Because of the time value of money, it usually makes more sense to pay taxes later rather than sooner whenever possible.

Paying taxes is the last in line. However, the last thing a CPA or other tax planner wants to do is call a client on April 15 and say, "By the way, you owe the IRS $100,000." Those calls are never fun for either party. The third objective of tax planning is to find out, as early as possible, what taxes will be owed and when they will have to be paid to give the client the time to plan.

We recently met with a new client who was seeking help in managing their new wealth, acquired as a result of the sale of their business. The client was a husband-and-wife team who had built a very profitable business. Like many business owners, they concentrated on the growth of their business and little else.

A year or so after the sale of their business, on April 15

their accountant at 4:00 p.m. presented them with their tax return and the tax bill to go with it for $1,000,000. They had no idea this tax bill was coming because the accountant never discussed tax planning or preparation. Part of the tax planning equation is preparation for the potential and impending tax bill. They were obviously in shock and had to scramble to come up with the money to pay the bill.

Tax planners who can tell clients in November and December what they will owe in April are doing their jobs well. Clients may not like what they hear, but at least they have been forewarned and can prepare. In many instances, knowing your "number" or tax liability in October, November, or December gives you the time to explore different tax mitigation strategies to reduce it and prepare to pay it.

YOUR NUMBER ONE EXPENSE

Most people don't really understand that taxes are one of the largest expenses they will face in their lifetimes, especially, but not only, if they are business owners. The problem is that most people think about taxes solely in terms of income taxes, which hardly covers the field.

The point is that when you start adding all these taxes up—income tax, payroll tax, sales tax, real property tax, personal property tax—you quickly come to realize how large a percentage of your income is going to taxes. The importance of tax planning now starts to come into focus. This also sheds light on the value of The VFO, made up of a team of professionals whose sole purpose is to assist you in managing your wealth, which includes mitigating your taxes.

Having drawn your attention to this unpleasant news, it's time to delve into some of the strategies that exist for legally eliminating or deferring taxes: the structures and strategies available when you're working with capable tax planners.

INSTALLMENT SALES TRUST

A VFO Installment Sales Trust is a strategy that can be used by any taxpayer facing large capital gains tax. It doesn't matter where that capital gain occurs. It could be from the sale of a business, real estate, highly appreciated stock, or artwork.

An installment sales trust is a trust you establish, managed by a trustee, that sells the appreciated assets or assets that you anticipate will appreciate. When you sell the assets to the trustee, the trustee gives you a note receivable. What you now own is the note receivable rather than the assets themselves. This permits you to defer paying taxes on the sale of the assets since the IRS distinguishes between an outright sale and an installment sale. You pay taxes on a capital gain only at the time you take money out of the trust, which you can do incrementally.

Any highly appreciated asset is eligible to be bought and sold through an installment sales trust. We'll look at what this specifically means for selling a business in Chapter 9.

OPPORTUNITY ZONES

The Tax Cuts and Jobs Act signed into law in 2017 establishes another means of deferring capital gains taxes by investing in "opportunity zones." Opportunity zones are specially designated, economically distressed areas in need of investment and rehabilitation. There are now hundreds of these funds investing in over 8,700 federally designated opportunity zone tracts across the United States. There are several tax advantages to investing capital gains in an opportunity zone.

Many commercial and residential areas throughout the country desperately need investment dollars. The U.S. Treasury Department went to the governors of each state and asked them to identify the areas in their states in need of redevelopment. The governors submitted lists of such areas, and the Treasury Department certified those that qualified as opportunity zones.

Not all properties in opportunity zones are necessarily what are thought of as "run-down areas." Some properties just happen to fall within zip codes the state government has identified in this manner. If you realize a capital gain, you have six months to invest that money in an opportunity zone in order to reap the investment's tax advantages. The first inducement is that an opportunity zone investment defers your capital gain taxes until 2026.

Although capital gains tax deferral is the first benefit of getting into an opportunity zone investment if you hold that investment, you don't have to pay capital gains tax until 2026. If you sell that investment before 2026, you'll need to pay capital gains tax when you do. The second and probably greatest benefit of an opportunity zone investment is that if you hold it for a minimum of ten years, you pay no capital gains tax at all on the profit you make when you sell the investment.

ROTH CONVERSIONS: LONG-TERM TAX PLANNING

Earlier on, we mentioned that there is this-year tax planning, next-year tax planning, and long-term tax planning. Let's look at an example of long-term planning.

First, you should realize that long-term tax planning may

increase your short-term tax liability. Although this may seem crazy at first, it actually makes good sense to give up a little today to get a lot back tomorrow. This is what happens with a Roth conversion.

If you have money in a regular IRA or 401(k) account transferred to an IRA, you'll pay income tax when you take money out of the account after you retire. You don't pay taxes if you take money out of a Roth IRA account because the money in a Roth IRA consists of after-tax dollars. With a regular IRA, you get tax deductions for the years you put money in.

There are several private investments, particularly in commercial and multifamily residential real estate, that offer an IRS-allowed discounted value when converting from a regular IRA into a Roth IRA. Say toward the end of one year, you invest $100,000 from a regular IRA in an investment property in the developmental stage. At the end of the year, the developer is required to have a third-party, independent appraisal done on the current value of the investment.

Then, early the following year, the custodian of your regular IRA is required to tell you the fair market value of your IRA on the last day of the previous year. The development you've invested in, however, is now just raw land, sticks, and bricks. The building or buildings haven't been built, and there are no tenants. As a result, the current fair market value of your investment may be as low as 50 percent of the original investment. In plain English: your $100,000 investment is now showing a tax valuation of $50,000 due to its incomplete status.

This is a powerful opportunity. You can convert the investment from a regular IRA to a Roth IRA and now pay taxes on a valuation of 50,000 rather than $100,000. Fast forward four or five years. The property has now been developed and the buildings sold off. Your original $100,000 investment could now potentially be worth $150,000—all of which, being in a Roth IRA, is now tax-free. With a Roth conversion, you're actually paying some tax dollars now because you want to save a lot of tax dollars in the future.

Another example would be if you own stocks in your IRA and some or all lose value due to market corrections, recession, or some other factor. Those values can be the basis for converting at a discount. For example, your original $100,000 stock portfolio within your IRA decreases in value to $60,000. You can convert or move your IRA portfolio to a Roth portfolio and pay tax on the $60,000 value. If those stocks recover or you sell them and purchase new investments, the growth will be tax-free.

Also, now that you have converted this asset to a Roth IRA, all future investments made after this asset's sale will grow tax-free. This conversion, it's important to note, is available to all IRA owners and is not subject to any income or other restrictions.

ADDITIONAL TAX MITIGATION STRATEGIES: ENERGY-RELATED INVESTMENT FUNDS

One of the relationships we enjoy as part of our VFO Model is a single-family office that has been involved in the oil and gas business for fifty years. They are a vertically integrated company that primarily drills gas wells within the Marcellus Shale in Pennsylvania. For that reason and their very strict adherence to remaining debt-free, they have provided our clients with an opportunity to invest in their investment funds.

Because of the energy tax-law advantages, under current law investors can write off approximately 75 percent of their investment in the first year and an additional 15 percent in the second year in an oil- and gas-related infrastructure development investment fund. Within a year of the fund's establishment, investors may also receive dividends which are eligible for a 15 percent discount on the distributed income.

The IRS allows oil and natural gas companies to write off

what is called intangible drilling costs (IDC). This means that approximately 80 percent of an investment in companies that do such drilling, like the natural-resources partner company described above, can be written off as nontaxable in the first year. Meaning that you're able to make an investment that also gives you a tax write-off.

This type of energy-related investment can offer a great opportunity to convert tax dollars to future partially tax-sheltered income. Due to the current drilling technology, these gas wells can produce gas and income for up to thirty-five to fifty years.

COST SEGREGATION

Cost segregation is a strategy for people who own commercial real estate, one of the principal alternative asset classes you can use to defer taxes. If you own a commercial office building and lease it out to someone else's company or even your own company, the building is depreciated over thirty-nine and a half years. However, you can accelerate depreciation on some parts of the building if they are properly identified and segregated.

The carpeting and window coverings in an office building, for instance, might have a five-year rather than an almost forty-year depreciation life span. The IRS also considers what cost-segregation experts call "qualified" electrical and plumbing to have a five- or seven-year life span. A cost-segregation study may also determine that the building's exterior assets, such as a parking lot, have a fifteen-year life span. A cost-segregation study that breaks a property down into these different parts can dramatically defer taxes by identifying more depreciation up front and less down the road.

A FINAL THOUGHT

The most important lesson here is that tax mitigation depends on this-year, next-year, and long-term tax planning. Plan ahead and always consult with your tax professionals. At the same time, there are a variety of strategies you likely want to consider to mitigate your taxes and, consequently, enhance your wealth. Aside from the ones in this chapter, there is private placement life insurance, which we will discuss in Chapter 11, and benefit-focused retirement plans, which we discussed in Chapter 6.

8

WHAT IS AN ASSET PROTECTION PLAN?

BY J. ALAN SOELBERG AND ROBERT ANNABLE

ENSURING YOUR WEALTH IS NOT TAKEN FROM YOU unjustly by litigants is the purpose of asset protection planning. As the wealthy are often targets of frivolous and unfounded lawsuits given their "deep pockets," high-performing virtual family offices are adept at asset protection planning. We live in a litigious society, and wealthy individuals and families are primary targets for lawsuits. It really can be a jungle out there, so a major concern of affluent families is protecting their wealth from potential lawsuits, litigants, creditors, and catastrophic loss. Of course, anyone can be sued, and the legal fees and other expenses needed to defend against even unfounded or nuisance lawsuits often involve financial loss.

THE ASSET PROTECTION STRESS TEST

Asset protection is a critical component of any wealth planning solution. You need to create barriers that will protect your wealth.

There are universal general principles behind any good asset protection plan, but these need to be adapted to individual needs. One way to get moving in the right direction is to take a four-step stress test of your current asset-protection plan or lack thereof. This stress test will help you determine how well your wealth is now shielded from frivolous or unfounded lawsuits and similar attacks.

The four steps in the asset-protection stress test are:

- **Step 1: Determine high-probability and significant risks:** What is likely to happen, and if it does happen, how detrimental will it be? This can be a rough estimate based on your experience or you can involve more sophisticated analysis and calculation.

- **Step 2: Determine your level of concern:**
  What are your needs, wants, and issues? For
  instance, if you are involved in a business whose
  products and services are cutting edge and
  experimental, your level of concern might be
  higher than if you own a more conventional
  business.

- **Step 3: Evaluate your current asset-
  protection plan:** Do you have a plan at all and if
  you do, is it adequate to your needs?

- **Step 4: Take appropriate action:** This may
  involve taking dramatic next steps or if all is well,
  no steps at all.

PROTECT YOUR WEALTH BY AVOIDING MISTAKES

Asset protection planning uses legally accepted strategies
to ensure your wealth is not taken from you unjustly. These
strategies can help avoid litigation entirely or can help
motivate an amicable settlement should litigation take
place.

Legitimate asset protection has nothing to do with hiding
assets or any other illegal or unethical practice. However,

asset protection can be a somewhat tricky business, so the best way to protect yourself is by avoiding pitfalls and mistakes.

There are five major mistakes affluent individuals and families often make that expose their assets to litigants, creditors, and other potentially devastating consequences:

- Starting to protect your assets when it is already too late

- Not having liability insurance

- Not integrating asset protection with your other wealth management strategies

- Being unsure of why you have made or are making important decisions

- Not seeking professional guidance

To help you protect your wealth as much as you can, let us look at how to avoid each of these mistakes in turn.

Starting Too Late

If you have not done so already, the time to start asset protection planning is *now*. The time *not* to start is once you are aware that a claim is or may be made against you.

The legal term for moving assets into a trust or other vehicle to protect them after you know or suspect a claim may be made against you is "fraudulent conveyance." In court, any attempt at fraudulent conveyance will be reversed and probably make a bad situation even worse.

Fraudulent conveyance comes in two varieties:

- **Actual fraud:** This involves actual intent. It occurs when someone transfers assets to a third party who is under their control or influence. This strategy is to make it seem that you no longer have the assets necessary to pay creditors or litigants, although those assets are actually still under your control.

- **Constructive fraud:** This involves the economics of a transfer of assets rather than the intent behind the transfer. If someone in financial difficulty transfers assets rapidly or precipitously, there may be a presumption of constructive fraud.

Determining intent is tricky since it is often impossible to know exactly what someone was thinking or intending. As a way of getting around this difficulty, courts look at circumstantial evidence or what is called "badges of fraud," which include the following:

- Current or likely litigation

- Transfer of assets to family members

- Transfers conducted secretly

The solution to this problem is to do asset protection planning before you need the protection. Do not delay. If you have not acted yet, act now.

No Liability Insurance

This mistake comes in a number of variations:

- No liability insurance

- Not enough liability insurance

- The wrong kind of liability insurance

This is a simple problem with a simple solution. Many individuals—even highly competent, successful business owners—have no or substandard liability insurance. They could benefit from larger umbrella liability policies, but neither they nor their insurance brokers have taken this into consideration. Certain insurance companies also limit the amount of liability coverage that can be provided.

Effective asset protection planning requires ensuring that you have the right kinds and amounts of liability insurance. Most people could, for instance, benefit from larger umbrella liability policies, but neither they nor their brokers think of or consider this. A further complication is that many, although not all, insurance companies limit the amount of liability insurance their brokers can provide.

The good news is that liability insurance is relatively inexpensive. You and the professionals you engage simply need to seek out the right insurer and the right policy. Business owners in particular might benefit from a higher-quality or more-customized directors and officers liability plan.

The first line of defense in an asset protection plan is to avoid lawsuits, although this is often out of your control. The second line of defense is adequate liability insurance. To determine if your liability insurance meets your needs, take or retake the stress test outlined earlier in this chapter. This should be done and redone at regular intervals to uncover and correct any gaps in coverage since circumstances are bound to change.

Not Integrating Asset Protection Planning with Other Wealth Management Strategies

As we have said many times, comprehensive wealth management and planning encompass all five major concerns, including estate planning and tax mitigation. Unfortunately, the various components of an overall strategy are often approached separately and independently, which is exactly the wrong way to do it.

For example, The VFO Advisory Group was specifically created to take a holistic approach to all aspects of wealth management, ensuring that all components of your financial life work together seamlessly. Such an approach leads to and includes an understanding of tradeoffs that are being made and risks that might otherwise have been overlooked.

A good example is gifting heirs. This might be good estate planning but could be considered a fraudulent conveyance when it comes to asset protection. Preventing such problems requires care and coordination that can only come with a wider perspective.

Placing inherited assets in a properly structured trust, for example, can protect them from creditors including divorcing spouses. Here, two of the five major concerns—estate planning and asset protection planning—have been made to work hand-in-hand. In almost every case, comprehensive wealth-management solutions are both more effective and more cost-effective than piecemeal ones.

Being Unsure of Why You Have Made or Are Making Important Decisions

Why have you made certain asset protection-planning decisions? What was your rationale, and what was the intended result? If you cannot answer these questions, there is a good chance that your asset protection planning will not deliver the actual protection you need. In a legal deposition, for instance, there is a strong possibility a court will be suspicious if you cannot give good answers to these questions.

There is an important proviso here, which is that you need to be able to answer such questions on a general, rather than specific, level. Asset protection planning can become quite complex if your financial and personal circumstances are complicated, as they often are with high-net-worth individuals.

You should be able to explain the reasoning behind the actions you have taken in broad terms, but you do not need to be an expert in the strategies and financial products that have been employed. That is up to the skilled professionals whose advice you have solicited and followed, which leads to the fifth asset-protection mistake you should avoid.

Not Seeking Professional Guidance

To protect your assets, as is the case in meeting all your wealth management needs, you need to work with skilled professionals. The problem is that many people who say they are asset protection planning professionals do not really have the expertise they claim.

Some of these so-called experts are pretenders who know just enough about asset protection strategies to get themselves and you into trouble. Others could be called predators because they prey on the fear of litigation but deliver ineffectual solutions. There is a third category, exploiters, who overcharge egregiously for asset protection solutions that may well be inappropriate. All these categories of so-called experts will end up doing you far more harm than good.

You need to work with a true authority in the field of asset protection planning, someone other financial professionals recognize as an expert. This goes hand-in-hand with integrating asset protection into a holistic wealth management strategy.

It is possible to escape the jungle out there by taking appropriate action.

9

WHAT ARE EXIT STRATEGIES?

BY VINCE ANNABLE

MANY OF THE MOST SUCCESSFUL INDIVIDUALS OR families created their wealth by being successful business owners. If you founded, are building, and intend to sell or transfer your business, your high-performing virtual family office has you covered.

We had a business that was a 50/50 partnership referred to us because they were involved in a possible sale to a private equity group. They had asked their CPA what the tax ramifications would be with this sale. As happens so often, the CPA said there was nothing they could do to mitigate the taxes, they should be excited about the sale and profits and pay the tax on their $30 million transaction. Not what you want to hear from your CPA.

The VFO group looked at the transaction and was able to structure the sale incorporating tax-mitigating strategies which significantly reduced their immediate taxes. We were able to eliminate and defer the majority of their tax liability. This is what a team of professionals can do when there is a coordinated effort to explore how to manage issues and solutions. All of these solutions are available in the tax code if you have a team who understands how to use the tax code to your benefit.

THE BUSINESS OWNER'S DILEMMA

If you're a business owner, your attention is sharply focused on running and growing your enterprise. Most of your assets are probably tied up in your business. The problem is that you may not have the bandwidth or expertise to manage your net worth so as to protect and maximize it for you and your family.

You, like most entrepreneurs, are probably building your business with the intention of selling it at a handsome profit someday. That may even be your retirement plan. However, you can't wait until the day before you decide to sell to say, "Okay, I'm going to sell my business tomorrow," if you don't want to give up a large percentage of your profit to taxes. You have to plan for the sale in advance. Selling your business requires preparing and executing an intricate transition process.

People generally build businesses for three reasons. One, they want to provide a good lifestyle for themselves and their families and, two, don't want to work for someone else. The best way to attain both goals is to build and grow a business of your own.

The third goal is to build your business for eventual sale at a considerable profit. As your business becomes more successful, you need to pay attention to the details of both your personal net worth and the business's value. You'll also want to be prepared for any unanticipated occurrences, including lawsuits or similar catastrophes that could threaten the security of your enterprise.

Welcome to the world of multitasking. Fortunately, you can now outsource this to a virtual family office and its team of experts. Of course, you'll remain intimately involved in planning, but you can now delegate important details and decisions with confidence. Your main focus will remain your business, as it should, but you'll have the other critical bases covered.

We're not talking only about business owners in the traditional sense here. Many if not most of the physicians, dentists, and similar professionals who build their own practices are also building businesses and need to plan their exit strategies.

BUSINESS AND PERSONAL ASSETS

One of the keys to planning an exit strategy is separating your business and personal assets while gradually transferring as many assets as possible from the business to the personal column. To repeat, business owners usually hold most of their assets in their enterprises. That may be necessary when first starting a business, but this approach can become increasingly self-defeating as the business grows.

Let's use a simple analogy. If you're a business owner, think of your financial life as being like a pair of pants. Say your business assets are in the front left pocket and your personal or individual assets are in the front right pocket. There are two pockets but one pair of pants: all your assets are in one pocket or the other.

The basic principle is, whenever possible, to move assets from the front left to the front right pocket—from the business to the personal side. Of course, it's a bit more complicated than that. You may need to move some assets to a side or back pocket, depending on which strategies, such as tax mitigation, are used to protect your personal wealth.

These are all different pockets in the same pair of pants. The money isn't being taken away but getting moved around so that you can keep as much of the profits you make as possible when selling your business. If you keep all your assets in your front left pocket, you may have to pay up to half your profits in tax when selling your business, and that's obviously what you want to avoid.

START EARLY

It's worth noting that moving assets from the operating business "pocket," where they are liabilities, to the personal "pocket," where they are protected, will also help preserve your assets in the shorter term. This also means that even though it's never too late to start exit planning, it's always better to start early.

Many VFO Advisory Group clients are business owners or independent professionals in their forties or fifties. They're relatively young and not thinking about how they're going to sell and get out of their businesses. An exit strategy may never cross their minds, but it should.

Actually, they should be thinking about an exit from

day one. When you start a business, to potentially maximize your personal wealth, you should immediately start considering how and when you will leave. Do you want to sell your business, making it your retirement plan? Do you want to turn it over to the next generation? If so, are there members of the next generation with both the desire and ability to take it over?

Keep in mind that if all your wealth is tied up in your business and something happens to it, there goes all your wealth. An underlying principle, here as elsewhere, is diversification. When possible, as a business owner, you need to consider taking some of the wealth and assets invested in the business and putting it into other investments or entities as soon as possible. Doing so will often give you greater long-term security.

These assets should be noncorrelated to the business just as your portfolio should include private investments noncorrelated to public markets (see the following chapter). Indeed, one of the best places to invest these assets is possibly in a personalized portfolio.

DON'T LET THIS HAPPEN TO YOU

Having an exit strategy in place and diversifying your assets through the years will likely protect you as a business owner. To drive the point home, let's take the example of a medical professional who has done very well financially, making between $500,000 and $1 million a year, year in and year out, for many years. A low year for him would probably be $600,000 in net income, and a really good year would be $1 million plus.

He's now in his early sixties and has no money set aside for retirement. Every penny he's earned throughout his career has been used to build and support a high-end lifestyle. He lives in a $2.5–$3-million home, on which he still has a $1 million mortgage. He has a nice second home, an upscale cabin in the country, with an equally healthy mortgage. He and his family are always going on wonderful vacations. All his earnings have gone to support this lifestyle.

This is an intelligent man who hasn't applied his smarts to thinking about retirement. He figures that he has a business he will be able to sell for $3 million to $4 million, so everything will be all right. Going through the numbers, however, brings home the fact that even if he sells the business for $4 million, that capital is not going to generate the $600,000 to $1 million in yearly income to which he's become accustomed.

This is a big wake-up call, and what he needs to wake up to is an even bigger nightmare. He realizes it's possible that, given market conditions, he may not be able to sell his practice for as much as he'd like. Since his sole asset is his business, he's going to be in a lot of trouble if he retires, as originally planned, in three years.

It's never too late to start doing things differently, but the timing is not in his favor. If the medical professional had begun benefiting from powerful wealth planning strategies five or ten years earlier, he may have been much better prepared for retirement without a dramatic reduction in lifestyle. For instance, he's been paying between $200,000 to $400,000 a year in income tax, which could have possibly been cut in half with the right tax planning strategies.

CAPTIVE INSURANCE COMPANIES

A wealth planning strategy business owners can use to eliminate or defer income tax prior to exit is using a captive insurance company. This is a complex subject, but we can address some of the highlights and basic principles here.

For some time, large businesses have been taking advantage of captive insurance companies. These are insurance companies the businesses themselves establish to cover or self-insure selected risks. Captive insurance companies enable large businesses to customize coverage to their individual needs and get greater control over insurance costs and claims handling. This customized insurance coverage allows a business to insure risks for which commercial insurance coverage is either unavailable or impractical.

In the past, establishing and maintaining a captive insurance company was cost prohibitive for any but the very largest companies. The good news is, this has changed. In 2008, the IRS issued a ruling that allows a core captive insurance company to be set up and then divided into semi-autonomous "cells," each of which is owned by different companies. Think of "captive cells" as a way for small and medium-sized businesses to work together to participate in the benefits of a captive insurance company at a fraction of the cost. For our purposes, we will refer to these captive cells as a captive insurance company.

Let's look at three of the captive insurance company's numerous benefits:

·   Captive insurance companies can save a business money on insurance premiums.

·   Captive insurance companies allow smaller businesses to insure against risks their other policies do not, and cannot, cover.

·   A business owner pays tax-deductible premiums from their regular operating company to the captive insurance company they also own.

The premiums paid to the captive insurance company are used to pay claims. However, premiums used to pay claims can also become the captive's profit. Best of all, this profit typically has a tax rate of 0 percent. This is not a tax loophole. Congress specifically set forth tax benefits that are typical of all insurance companies for captive insurance companies, allowing them to accumulate premiums and reserves to pay claims. These benefits allow insurance companies, including captive insurance companies, to build insurance reserves. At the same time, business owners can build real assets in the captive insurance companies they also own.

A captive insurance company is sometimes compared to a type of retirement plan without all the rules and restrictions, but this appealing comparison is too simplistic. Business owners do get a tax deduction while building the asset, just as they do when building a retirement plan. The key difference is that the assets in a captive insurance company covers real business risks, which a retirement plan does not.

There are several reasons this asset can be a key component of a business owner's long-term financial well-being. First, the tax deductions for the operating company and the tax-free treatment of the captive insurance company's profits are an efficient way to build insurance reserves. Second, when the insured operating company has a loss covered by the captive, these insurance reserves will be available to pay the claim, which is very helpful when needed. In the case of a large or catastrophic business-casualty loss, these insurance reserves can save the enterprise. Third, as previously mentioned, a captive can build value over time, which will be available to the business owner upon eventual exit from the business.

THE DOMESTIC INTERNATIONAL SALES CORPORATION

A domestic international sales corporation, or DISC, which is sometimes referred to as a foreign sales corporation, is another structure that can eliminate business taxes. A DISC allows businesses with international sales to eliminate certain taxes on export income.

If your business exports products or services internationally, a DISC can help eliminate a large portion of US tax on this income. The Internal Revenue Code gives significant tax incentives for export activities to domestic corporations—that is, business enterprises incorporated in the United States. DISC shareholders, such as business owners, benefit from greatly reduced income tax rates on the income earned from certain exports of US-produced goods. If your business exports goods internationally, you would benefit from the advice on creating a DISC available through the expert team at your high-performing virtual family office.

THE VFO INSTALLMENT TRUST

An installment sales trust is an important tax-deferment strategy discussed in the previous chapter. It's also a good tool to use when planning and executing a business exit. The proceeds from a sale can be put in an installment trust, which has several advantages, beginning with tax deferment.

In a recent case, a business owner who had just sold his business would have had to pay $600,000 in taxes if the profits from the sale had not been put in an installment trust. An installment trust doesn't eliminate this tax, but because it defers it, that $600,000 can now be invested along with the former business owner's other assets. Taxes can be deferred and the return from the investment realized for any number of years. In some cases, tax can even be eliminated if the trust remains in place after the owner's death since the assets in the trust will then pass on to the business owner's beneficiaries. An installment trust's main purpose in an exit strategy is as a tax-deferral strategy.

MORE EXIT STRATEGIES?

The business exit strategies you've just learned about are illustrative rather than exhaustive. The VFO Model provides access to tax, insurance, and pension experts who have devoted their entire careers to utilizing established and innovative new business-owner wealth-preservation strategies.

Another strategy is utilizing the tax advantages of hiring your own children. You can pay them through your company payroll, and they can then invest that money in an IRA. That means you can write off what you paid them, and they can write off what they put into their IRAs. Taxes are significantly deferred or eliminated, creating another way for you to pass money from your business to your children. Keep in mind that when you hire your children, they are employees and need to be working in the business.

The takeaway here is that if you are a business owner, you should always plan for and keep your exit strategy in mind. It may never be too late to plan, but earlier is always better.

Also bear in mind that your exit strategy will keep changing and evolving. Times change, tax laws change, and the economic environment changes. The earlier you begin planning your exit strategy, the more it may change over time, and this should be seen as a net positive since it increases your level of control.

10

WHAT ARE ALTERNATIVE INVESTMENTS?

BY VINCE ANNABLE AND ROBERT ANNABLE

LIKE SINGLE-FAMILY OFFICES, HIGH-PERFORMING virtual family offices often include a team of investment management experts. And like a great many single-family offices, this team will often consist of those who understand and include alternative investments in the overall portfolio design. In fact, the ability to deliver well-vetted alternative investment solutions is characteristic of high-performing virtual family offices.

Blackstone Group, one of the largest private equity firms and providers of alternative-asset investment solutions, defines alternative investments as:

Investment categories other than traditional securities or long-only stock and bond portfolios; including hedge funds, venture capital, private equity, private credit, and real estate.

The key point here is that, in principle, alternative investments are not correlated to the movement of the public markets because they are private nontraded securities. They do not have the same volatility or daily swings as the public markets. Private alternative investments also help protect you from yourself and the herd mentality.

When the markets are flying high, investors typically jump in when they are near the top because now they have seen everyone buying in. The fear of missing out, FOMO, takes over. Next comes the major corrections in the market, and investors watch the herd selling and driving down the markets, so out of fear, they sell. And of course the cycle repeats and you feel like you're on a roller coaster.

Alternative private investments, in principle, do not participate in market volatility, so investors are protected from the herd and their emotional selves. Think of it this way:

if the stock market drops 1 percent, 5 percent, 10 percent, or more, do you see the value of your home or other real estate investments or other private investments doing the same? No, you do not run to your real estate broker when the stock market falls and tell them to sell your house or other real estate investments immediately. If you own private stock in a healthcare research firm that is creating a cure for cancer, does it drop in value just because the stock market falls.

These emotional decisions may often cause portfolio underperformance, and if your entire portfolio is based on some variation of the old 60/40 model and in totally liquid market investments, you may experience very negative returns. However, if a portion of your portfolio is in alternative nontraded investments not affected by the volatility, this smooths out the ride on that roller coaster of volatility.

Research in JP Morgan Asset Management revealed that allocating just 30 percent to alternatives in your portfolio can substantially increase your annual returns, while simultaneously strengthening stability and decreasing risk.

Most investors have been receiving the same investment advice for the last seventy-plus years, which is to invest 60 percent in stocks and 40 percent in bonds—the modern portfolio theory. In our opinion, this advice is right out of the Jurassic era. Just as cigarette companies in the 1950s ran ads with physicians recommending Camel cigarettes, the modern portfolio theory was created on a false premise. You have likely noticed physicians are no longer recommending cigarettes, but there are some financial advisors today who are still recommending the 60/40 model.

THE ILLIQUIDITY PREMIUM

The use of alternative investments in your investment portfolio provides you with less volatility in your overall portfolio with the potential to mitigate risk and provide higher returns. This is sometimes referred to as the illiquidity premium.

"Illiquidity" and "market inefficiencies" sound fairly negative. Counterintuitively, when it comes to making the greatest return on your investment, the opposite can turn out to be the case.

Looking back to the markets in 2000–2001, 2006–2008, and our more recent bull market 2020–2022, we saw knee-jerk FOMO reactions to the markets. Many investors bought when the markets were at their highest and sold when the market was at its lowest, hoping to "save" what was left, driven by FOMO and the herd mentality.

The same was true of many large financial institutions and mutual funds. Even when the people at the helm knew better—and let us hope at least some of them did—they were forced to liquidate holdings at the worst possible time because in many cases, their charters forced them to. A great example of this was what happened in 2008.

By the time the market started turning around in late 2009, it was too late to recoup losses. The money had already gone down the drain, in large part because of so-called market efficiencies. An "efficient market" is one that rapidly reflects and adjusts to changing facts on the ground. In general, in an efficient market, securities are neither under- nor over-valued. They are priced in a way that reflects all relevant available information.

Market efficiency and liquidity go hand-in-hand. In an efficient market, you can easily buy low and sell high. The problem is that it is just as easy to buy high and sell low. In fact, it is all too simple to push the panic button when the market's roller coaster accelerates from a peak down into a valley.

Illiquidity and inefficient markets can potentially save some investors from themselves.

To take a simple example, an investment in privately held commercial real estate requires a long-term commitment of capital, often five years or more. If you think you need your money back in two years, you are basically out of luck—which turns out to be lucky in some cases. Therefore, when looking at these types of investments, your advisor needs to know your liquidity needs and plan accordingly when constructing your portfolio.

To put this in more formal financial terms, the potentially higher returns attributed to alternative, in contrast to conventional, investments may be attributed to the "illiquidity premium." Although several factors are at play, the more liquid an investment is, typically the less risk is involved and the lower the return. The standard risk/reward equation, with which you may be familiar, comes into play. The higher the risk, the higher the reward for success because the chance of failure is comparably high. Much has been written about the illiquidity premium, and the subject can be extensively researched.

To be clear, in an efficient public market, information is available in real time and assets can be traded immediately. This creates a relatively uniform market in which most investors have equal chances of profit and loss. Public markets are transparent because it is illegal to trade on insider information. This market transparency delivers returns that are "symmetric"—more or less the same—for most investors.

Private markets and private investments operate with an

entirely different set of rules. Private companies are not required to disclose corporate information to the public. So-called insider trading is not illegal but rather the name of the game. As a result, investors in these companies have greater or "asymmetric" access to information about company management, company financials, sales pipelines, and strategies.

In short, market inefficiencies can give patient investors—those willing and who have the financial ability to wait long enough to make illiquid investments—advantages and opportunities over investors in publicly traded, highly liquid markets.

WHY ALTERNATIVES?

There are a number of reasons for you to incorporate alternatives into your investment portfolio. The following are a few of those reasons:

· Rising interest rates

· Higher levels of inflation

· Heightened geopolitical risks

· Slower real economic growth

It is widely believed a different approach to portfolio construction is needed, including a reexamination of the merits of the 60/40 allocation. The traditional 60/40 model is an antiquated attempt at capturing a balanced portfolio.

When modern portfolio theory was first implemented, bonds provided a real return and an opportunity to hedge the effects of a falling stock market. Now, however, bonds can no longer reliably serve as the shock absorbers or diversifiers that they were originally intended to do. Alternative investments in private floating rate credit can take the place of part of that bond allocation. In addition to the benefits of the floating rate feature, they can offer higher sources of income.

The addition of alternative investments can offer a customized portfolio designed to enhance returns, diversify risk, and supplement income. Due to the low interest rates available today, income from bonds is not a value add. Portfolio diversification is the why. Today's markets are not the markets many grew up with in the '80s, '90s, or 2000s. Today's markets demand proper diversification in liquid and illiquid assets to ensure an overall balance and reduced volatility, thereby mitigating the risk and creating the opportunity to increase the returns.

DUE DILIGENCE OF ALTERNATIVE INVESTMENTS

The importance of allocating to alternative investments is well substantiated at this point based on this year's market, the state of the economy producing slower real economic growth, higher interest rates, record-high inflation, and of course those nagging geopolitical risks. Due to the increased focus on including alternatives in a portfolio, it is important to understand not all alternatives are created equal. They must be examined thoroughly before they are ever offered to a client. We will now look at that process.

Alternatives to be properly allocated to, and included in investment portfolios, should be properly analyzed and studied. We require a detailed due diligence review to be conducted before investments are made. The following is the guideline we follow and recommend before a particular alternative is accepted into our program:

- We need to get to know the principals, their experience, the reason behind why they are in business, and how many programs they have completed.

- We determine the economic value being provided. We examine the economic cycle to evaluate the investment potential and demand.

- We ascertain the financial strength of the investment, including how the investment is structured financially. How much money is raised as capital, and how much is borrowed?

- We evaluate the personnel, including their experience, commitment, and attitude in order to understand what to expect during the fundraising period, operations, and how they will address client service issues.

- We look at the fund's ability to raise capital, taking into account its distribution team and their previous successes or failures. It is essential to successfully raise the necessary funds in a timely manner.

- We always consider the various risk factors and how our clients can mitigate them or at the very least, understand and accept them.

- We calculate the total expenses of the program, including both up-front and back-end costs. Each alternative offering must properly disclose its selling, marketing, and operating expenses in its offering documents.

- We take into account third-party reports and results. Most alternative investment sponsors use reputable third-party law firms whose specialization is to review all aspects of a private placement.

In sum, the due diligence process can take several months. It is important that the process is documented properly. In addition to the due diligence, the program/product should be analyzed for the level of risk, income, growth, time to maturity, and overall success. The product would be given a score to represent these measures. The attributes of an alternative investment can help a client achieve investment goals. Income, growth, and tax benefits can all be achieved by properly using well-researched and vetted alternatives.

11

WHAT IS PRIVATE PLACEMENT LIFE INSURANCE?

BY FRANK V. SENECO AND VINCE ANNABLE

PRIVATE PLACEMENT LIFE INSURANCE (PPLI) IS somewhat of a mainstay among many single-family offices. For the wealthy who qualify, PPLI can be a very powerful solution. All high-performing virtual family offices are able to provide PPLI for their clients who can benefit and fit the criteria.

Consider this case study:

Susan is fifty-nine years old, residing in California. She recently sold her company for a large sum and now wants to invest $25 million to benefit her and her family. Although she does not need the money in the future, she wanted to be able to access it if necessary. Susan wants her money to grow an average of 6 percent per year. Her blended tax rate is about 54 percent.

If she chooses taxable investments and invests $5 million a year for five years, she will have an after-tax account balance of about $44 million after twenty-five years. However, if Susan places $5 million a year for five years in a PPLI policy that performs like taxable investments, she will have an account balance of about $79 million after twenty-five years. She will be able to access the funds through tax-free withdrawals and policy loans.

At the same time, the PPLI policy is integrated into her estate plan. Although the death benefit from the insurance will change, it is about $63 million.

For many, smart investing is a cornerstone of building significant wealth. Therefore, maximizing returns is key. Aside from investing in strategies or with managers that produce superior returns, efficient investing by reducing fees and taxes produces superior results. It is not only what you make; it is what you keep. Taxes and fees can turn superior investment returns into mediocre investments. At the same time, to build significant wealth, the ability to synergistically combine tax-efficient investing and wealth planning can be extremely powerful.

For over the past thirty-five-plus years, many of the world's wealthiest families have incorporated a specialized strategy into their wealth planning to meaningfully increase returns by negating taxes. This specialized strategy also plays an important role in addressing a variety of wealth planning concerns.

The strategy is called private placement life insurance which is commonly known as PPLI. The strategy is very versatile and can be structured in the United States or abroad to meet a client's or family's particular investment and wealth planning goals.

WHAT IS PPLI?

Technically, PPLI is the use of an institutional customized life insurance solution that uses the tax benefits afforded to life insurance to one or more investment funds, or a customized investment portfolio. To be clear, PPLI is life insurance. It is NOT a tax dodge. In the hands of capable professionals, PPLI provides considerable wealth planning advantages—and that is the focus. PPLI is part of a larger wealth planning agenda.

Take a tax-inefficient investment and use it within PPLI—the investment can grow tax deferred, be accessed tax-free via policy withdrawals and loans, and be passed to heirs as part of an income-tax-free death benefit. PPLI can also be used in a variety of business situations such as paying for corporate benefits.

PPLI differs from traditional life insurance in several ways. First, PPLI permits each of the professionals in the transaction to carry out the function for which they are best suited instead of the life insurance company handling all aspects. For instance, with a retail policy such as whole life or universal life policy, the insurer accepts and holds the premium in its general account. The retail insurer makes investment decisions about how to invest the premium and retains most or all of the death benefit risk. Policy assets in the insurance company's general account are subject to the claims of the insurer's creditors.

Conversely, with PPLI, as a version of variable insurance, the insurer holds a policy's premium in an account that is separate and segregated from its general account and where it is not reachable by the insurer's creditors. This layer of creditor protection and the knowledge that the financial performance of the policy's investments is not dependent on the financial decisions of the insurer is a top reason why PPLI is so attractive to wealthy individuals.

Another attribute unique to PPLI over retail policies is the insurance company's acceptance of the policyholder's choice of investment manager and custodian. The investment decisions are made by professionals designated by the policyholder and not the insurance company.

The benefits of PPLI can be summarized as follows:

· Tax-deferred accumulation of cash value

· Tax-free withdrawals and loans

· Income-tax-free death benefit

· Client choice of investment manager and custodian

· Customized investment options

· Institutional pricing

· The ability to majorly enhance wealth planning

PPLI is about enhancing investments by adding tax efficiency with an insurance element to provide wealth planning certainty. PPLI can also be creatively used to enable policyholders to get their desired outcomes. For example, many of the wealthy are thinking about creating family dynasties. By adroitly combining dynasty trusts and PPLI, a large percentage of these families are well positioned to create the wealth to sustain and grow a family dynasty.

WHO CAN BENEFIT FROM PPLI?

PPLI is reserved exclusively for an accredited investor or qualified purchaser. These are individuals or entities who are allowed to deal, trade, and invest in financial securities and satisfy one or more requirements regarding income, net worth, asset size, or professional experience. The rationale for this criterion is that PPLI enables policyholders to take advantage of investment products not available in retail insurance, such as private equity and hedge funds, and defer (or potentially eliminate) all the income tax that would otherwise have been paid on the realized gains on those assets. This results in policyholders having the ability to invest in a completely tax-free environment.

As noted, PPLI enhances investment returns and is used to deliver additional benefits as part of a client's wealth planning. For instance, PPLI is increasingly being used by wealthy families to transfer wealth more efficiently by combining an investment strategy with more sophisticated estate planning. By incorporating PPLI into a multigenerational trust structure, a family can defer or eliminate taxation on the investments underlying the policy. Upon the passing of the insured, the policy's income-tax-free death benefit essentially provides a step-up in basis at death for the underlying investments.

Businesses and single-family offices use PPLI to informally fund executive benefit programs, support business succession planning, and key person retention programs as well as invest institutional capital most efficiently. When institutions use PPLI correctly, the death benefit can be utilized to recover the costs of employee benefit programs, including the time value of money.

RULES OF THE ROAD

Two main rules must be adhered to with a PPLI policy: the diversification rule and the investor control rule.

Diversification Rule

In general, a policy must be diversified with at least five investments with the following percentages:

- No more than 55 percent of the value of the total assets of the account is represented by any one investment.

- No more than 70 percent of the value of the total assets of the account is represented by any two investments.

- No more than 80 percent of the value of the total assets of the account is represented by any three investments.

- No more than 90 percent of the value of the total assets of the account is represented by any four investments.

Investor Control Rule

Assets invested in a PPLI must be managed on a discretionary basis by the fund or an investment manager. Specifically, the policyholder is prohibited from making investment decisions. The policyholder may not select or recommend particular investments or investment strategies. All investment decisions must be made by the investment manager. A violation of this rule will negate all the tax benefits provided by the policy. However, the policy owner may pick the investment theme or style and can change the investment manager at will.

Some professionals try to circumvent these rules. Doing so can be easily avoided and is a very bad mistake.

CAVEAT

PPLI is being extensively used by the super-rich and their single-family offices. They are aiming to significantly grow their wealth as well as efficiently transfer their fortunes across the generations. More and more, PPLI is being used by those less affluent but still meeting the income or net worth criteria. The complication is that many professionals mistakenly:

- **Promote PPLI as a tax shelter:** PPLI is NOT an investment tax blocker. Yes, it can be used to mitigate taxes, but when integrated into an individual's or family's wealth planning, there is often a multitude of benefits accrued.

- **Cross over into the gray zone:** PPLI must always be a bright line transaction from how it fits into wealth planning to what investments are being used to the fact that the policyholder is not sneakily making investment decisions. What is sometimes called aggressive planning can easily result in severe complications for policyholders.

To get the benefits of PPLI without possible future adverse outcomes, therefore, requires working with professionals who have integrity, are experienced with PPLI, and make a concerted effort to understand how to make it work for the wealthy.

12

WHAT IS CONCIERGE MEDICINE?

BY DANIEL CARLIN, MD

HIGH-PERFORMING VIRTUAL FAMILY OFFICES commonly address the concerns of wealthy individuals and families beyond their financial concerns. A major concern of the wealthy is healthcare. A high-performing virtual family office can, when appropriate, bring a high-quality concierge medical practice to their wealthy client who would benefit. The following examples show what concierge medicine can look like.

A fifty-five-year-old business owner completed his executive physical, but given his family history of early heart disease, a special panel of cardiac biomarkers was added to the standard exam. Although the exam results were entirely normal, the biomarkers revealed an ongoing vascular injury and the beginning of arterial plaque formation. Under the guidance of a consulting cardiologist at WorldClinic, an internationally renowned concierge medical practice, the business owner's blood pressure and cholesterol medication was changed, and the probable culprit, dairy fat, was eliminated from his diet— to the chagrin of the business owner. The biomarker panel was repeated 120 days later and all evidence of the active vascular injury was resolved. Follow-up bloodwork, taken twice a year, indicated sustained success in mitigating this long-term risk.

A forty-six-year-old business owner felt a burning pain in his lower back the night before a critical industry speech. Convinced he had a kidney stone, he called the WorldClinic physician hotline. A four-minute interview and guided exam via FaceTime video revealed the diagnosis, an acute outbreak of lumbar shingles. He was immediately treated with medication from the WorldClinic personal prescription medical kit. The WorldClinic care team tracked his progress, and his case was resolved three weeks later. As a result of the immediate diagnosis and treatment, there was zero downtime for this busy executive.

One hour after a minor car accident, the driver began complaining of mild neck pain and tingling in his right thumb and index finger. His spouse called and talked with a World-Clinic on-duty emergency physician. In a five-minute interview, she described the situation and carried out a simple guided physical exam, which confirmed possible significant nerve injury. She was immediately guided to immobilize her husband's neck while transportation was arranged to a designated hospital with a verified CT scanner and a qualified radiological team. WorldClinic physicians contacted the emergency room in advance and relayed their concerns requesting an immediate CT scan of the husband's spine. It revealed a lateral fracture of the fourth cervical vertebrae, soon stabilized with a rigid neck brace. He made a full recovery and suffered no permanent neurological damage.

There's a famous saying that goes:

When you have your health, you have many problems.

When you don't have your health, you have one problem.

We can expand this idea to the people we love and care about.

It does not matter how rich you are, how famous you are, or how well-connected you are. For almost everyone, when you're sick or injured, all you want is to be healthy. And for most people, the same perspective extends to their children, spouses, other family members, and friends.

A truism in life is that ill health, at some point, is inevitable. Even the most careful individuals have accidents. Diseases from cancer to strokes and from neurological disorders to severe infections can beset anyone. There is no way to absolutely avoid healthcare problems and crises. However, as we will discuss when we address longevity planning, there are ways to mitigate some of the possibilities.

With healthcare institutions throughout the world increasingly stressed, people with financial resources are progressively not inclined to rely on these public systems—at least not in the ways most people rely on them. Instead, these individuals and families are more and more able and likely to pay for a higher standard of healthcare. The term for this is ***concierge medicine*** or ***concierge healthcare***.

Concierge medicine is an umbrella term used to describe a number of different retainer arrangements between a primary care physician and a patient. All the various forms of concierge medicine represent a return to privatizing primary healthcare. It is a way to get a higher quality of care where you and your loved ones are, and remain, center stage.

WHY DO PEOPLE SIGN UP FOR CONCIERGE MEDICINE?

Generally speaking, with the problems embedded in traditional primary healthcare systems acting as a backdrop, there are four primary, interconnected reasons people become patients of concierge medical practices:

- **They need to better deal with current healthcare concerns for themselves or their loved ones.** All of us will eventually be diagnosed with a serious or complex condition, or an event that will trigger a variety of healthcare concerns. The foremost of which concerns is where do they get the best medical care?

- **They are uncomfortable with the quality of the traditional primary medical care that is available.** Even though they may not have yet experienced a serious problem, they want to make sure they have high-caliber physicians and medical facilities for themselves and loved ones whenever the need arises and they recognize the considerable limitations of the traditional primary care medical system.

- **Their primary care physician is transitioning his or her practice to concierge medicine.** Although there are sometimes financial incentives for established physicians to become concierge medical physicians, the core motivation tends to be the ability to deliver superior patient care.

- **They want to live a very long and relatively malady-free life and want the same for their loved ones.** Advances in medicine are increasingly extending people's life spans, and this is a trend that is likely to accelerate. Proactively taking steps to live a long life sans illness is referred to as longevity planning.

It is very telling that patients who join a concierge medical practice because of a need to get better medical care or unease with the traditional healthcare system also tend to gravitate to longevity planning whenever possible. The same is the case for patients who follow their physician as he or she transitions to a concierge medical practice.

SERVICES OF CONCIERGE MEDICAL PRACTICES

In evaluating the field of concierge medicine, there are a number of deliverables that are often cited to separate it from the more "traditional" delivery of medicine. Then again, not every concierge medical practice will provide all of the possible services. The following are some of the more common services of concierge medical practices.

24/7 immediate on-call physicians: Getting access to a physician whenever medical services are required is the cornerstone of many higher-end concierge medical practices. Quick access to a high-caliber physician for timely diagnosis and immediate treatment saves lives and prevents acute problems from becoming critical.

Second opinion: Medicine is both a science and an art. Very often, it is about having access to vetted and recognized field-leading specialists for serious and complex diseases such as cancer and Parkinsonism. The ability to get high-quality second opinions for verification or for a different perspective is often a crucial resource provided by medical practices.

Secure 24/7 access to medical records: Especially in times of emergency, being able to immediately obtain medical information about a person can be crucial. What is also essential is that a patient's medical records cannot be sourced unless there is a healthcare emergency or by designated physicians.

Longevity planning: It is possible to lengthen a person's life span thanks to advances in genomics and by using a formal longevity protocol. Not only can people live longer, but they can also maintain a very high quality of life. Consequently, there is considerable demand for such expertise.

Access to leading specialists and medical centers: When specialists need to be consulted, the ability to be able to connect with leading authorities and the medical centers where they work can be lifesaving. Having knowledge of and access to these experts—wherever they are in the country or in the world—is an important component of many concierge medical practices.

Connected monitoring: With the adoption of smartphones and similar technologies, the ability to monitor a patient's health at a distance is becoming normative. Basically, such monitoring delivers a lot more data on which to base better decisions and create better outcomes. Connected monitoring is often the best way to manage a chronic condition.

Tele-diagnosis and treatment: Related to connected care, and often the cornerstone to 24/7 immediate on-call physicians, is the ability to use mobile technology to evaluate and treat patients. As the technology evolves, the range and quality of diagnosis and treatment will do so as well. The key to success in this endeavor is having the right tools for both the doctor and their distant patient.

Destination medical planning: For individuals and families who travel, knowing that reliable medical resources are locally available in different geographies is very worthwhile. Foreknowledge of medical resources can be lifesaving in the case of a medical crisis like a heart attack or major trauma. This becomes all the more important when people are traveling internationally, especially in foreign lands where the level of medical care might not be comparable to what they are accustomed to.

Foreign physician/hospital database: Across the world, the quality of a local physician's competence varies wildly. This is an important issue when a patient is visiting multiple destinations over a brief period of time and an illness starts in one city and continues as the patient travels.

Global medical evacuation: For families and individuals who travel abroad, the ability to have a fully insured evacuation plan to bring them home if they are hospitalized overseas is quite appealing. Historically, evacuation insurance has been bundled into travel assistance programs that included everything from eyeglass repair to physician-finding services. For the most part, they are insurance policies.

Personal medical resources: Starting effective treatment immediately with medication from a personalized medical resource like a prescription medical kit saves time and dramatically improves the outcome in a crisis like chest pain or an overwhelming allergic reaction, both of which can occur anytime without warning.

THE FUTURE OF CONCIERGE MEDICINE

There is little question that concierge medicine is a growth industry. Just consider the following equation incorporating several of the most recent and sustained trends in healthcare:

An increasingly turbulent healthcare system that is often ineffectively delivering on the promise of quality patient care

+

An increasing number of primary care physicians rejecting the current physician-employee practice model to restore the time and commitment they want to have in caring for their patients

+

New, sometimes hard-to-access, lifesaving technologies

+

An expanding cohort of potential patients that can both afford and are willing to pay for exceptional healthcare

---

A substantial and enduring yearly increase in the number of concierge medical practices

Although this concierge practice trend started among independent community physicians, it is very telling that it has now spread to the primary care staff of major medical centers. They recognize that this movement is not going away and are now actively seeking to lock in these patients for a variety of reasons.

Practicing physicians and smaller medical institutions are driving most concierge healthcare today. However, there are strong indications that many hospitals have begun establishing their own concierge medical practices. The economic and professional rationale for hospitals to offer concierge medical services that parallel those of many primary care physicians is their desire to be financially rewarded for superior clinical performance.

People are going to want new and innovative medical treatments such as immunotherapy to treat cancer, and they will always be willing to pay whatever they need to in order to receive the treatments. Moreover, they also want to know what diseases or illnesses are most likely to befall them in the future. Fortunately, their own genome can be analyzed to answer this question. Even more fortunately, once these possible future problems are identified, appropriate financial planning can occur in advance to eventually mitigate the cost of the best care for that particular problem.

For many people, the promise of concierge medicine is a longer life span. Longevity planning is becoming a major reason for joining a concierge medical practice. From being able to address acute and chronic health issues to taking preventive actions to leveraging the latest technologies, the result is a much longer and healthier life. The idea of living a long and fruitful life is very appealing. And for many people, concierge medicine will likely be instrumental to achieve this goal. Your high-performing virtual family office can connect you with the best leading concierge medical practice.

CODA

CHOOSING WISELY

FOR MANY SUCCESSFUL AND WEALTHY INDIVIDUALS and families, a virtual family office is the best type of firm to optimize their financial and personal lives. When implemented well, a virtual family office duplicates the advantages that high-performing single-family offices deliver to the super-rich.

The caveat is that you need to select and take an active role in managing your relationship with your high-performing virtual family office. We strongly recommend that you are involved and assertive, for this is the best way to get superior results.

To be clear,

Being able to most efficaciously and cost-effectively achieve your goals and deal with your concerns

+

Ensuring you're not missing out on major opportunities

Superior results

Operationally, this means you have to ask questions to ensure you are selecting and working with a high-performing virtual family office. There is often a lot of information to look for to make certain you are working with a high-performing virtual family office. To just touch on what you might want to know when it comes to the experts that are aligned with your high-performing virtual family office, consider the following questions you can ask the virtual family office professionals about the experts they are bringing to the table.

What specialized knowledge and skills does each expert have?

In your high-performing virtual family office, each expert needs to have a high level of niche specialization. They have to be extremely good in their field.

A good follow-up question is:

How did you determine if each expert is extremely good in his or her field?

You want your virtual family office professionals to explain how they chose and vetted the specialists. Another question that can be very helpful is:

Why is the expert in-house or external?

You want to know the logic as to why the expert is an employee of the virtual family office as opposed to going to an external expert. Keep in mind that by design, with a virtual family office, most of the experts are external.

Another possible question is:

How do the experts work cooperatively on your behalf?

Here, you are looking for an explanation of the methodologies that are in place to enable your team of experts to share ideas and recommendations.

And you always want to know:

How is each expert compensated?

In order for you to optimize your financial and personal

lives as well as those of your loved ones, you have to choose a high-performing virtual family office, and critically, you have to be in control.

ABOUT THE AUTHORS

RUSS ALAN PRINCE is the Executive Director of Private Wealth magazine (pw-mag.com) and Chief Content Officer for High-Net-Worth Genius (hnwgenius.com). He consults with family offices, the wealthy, fast-tracking entrepreneurs, and select professionals. He is the author or co-author of more than sixty-five books, including *Everyone Wins! How You Can Enhance and Optimize Business Relationships Just Like Ultra-Wealthy Entrepreneurs* and *How to Build a High-Performing Single-Family Office: Guidelines for Family Members and Senior Executives*. Collectively, the cache of research-based insights within Prince's publications is the most complete empirical analysis in the field and the largest, most comprehensive database on the topic.

VINCE ANNABLE, who grew up in Southern California, spent his youth enjoying all Southern California had to offer, joined the air force, and returned home after serving. He wondered what was next. He entered the financial services business in 1981 and created Wealth Strategies Advisory Group in 2009. He's also the proud author and creator of *The Household Endowment Model* (THEM), an investment and wealth-planning platform that he created based on Yale University's successful endowment fund investment strategy and the elite wealth-planning strategies employed by other wealth planning experts he has consulted with. He is also the founder and creator of The VFO Advisory Group, the high-performing virtual family office about which this book is written.

ABOUT PRIVATE WEALTH

Private Wealth (pw-mag.com): Advising the Exceptionally Affluent is the premier resource for leading professionals focused on meeting the financial, legal, and lifestyle demands of ultra-high-net-worth individuals and families, including the super-rich (net worth = US$500 million or more) and their single-family offices. The cohort that comprises the exceptionally affluent is larger now than at any time in history and is growing faster than at any time in history. A rapidly expanding majority of the exceptionally affluent, because of their substantial financial resources and often complex lives, require and desire extensive expert advice, support, and solutions to best achieve their desires and goals. And they need professionals to deftly address their concerns.

Private Wealth delivers state-of-the-art perspectives and insights on the exceptionally affluent and the leading professionals who serve them. The strategic and tactical content is fundamentally about delivering *exceptional value* to ultra-high-net-worth individuals and families. The information in Private Wealth can therefore be instrumental in helping leading professionals to build highly successful practices and businesses that, first and foremost, significantly benefit the exceptionally affluent.

Unique content is drawn from extensive practical experience and cutting-edge empirical studies. By design, a very sizable percentage of the content is highly actionable, enabling leading professionals to more powerfully connect with the exceptionally affluent and more capably assist them to achieve their agendas.

While Private Wealth is primarily intended for the broad array of experts who desire to better connect with and serve the exceptionally affluent, based on our ten-year experience (2008–2018) with the print version, a sizable percentage of ultra-high-net-worth individuals and families, including single-family office senior executives, will avail themselves of much of the content. Because of the interest the exceptionally affluent have in the material, we are thoughtful about including content that will help empower them to more productively optimize their lives and the lives of their loved ones.

ABOUT HIGH-NET-WORTH GENIUS

High-Net-Worth Genius (HNWgenius.com) is the premier resource to empower leading professionals to meet the financial, legal, and lifestyle demands of high-net-worth individuals and families. In addition, there are resources available for high-net-worth individuals and families to help them increasingly optimize their financial and personal lives as well as the lives of their loved ones.

By delivering superior results, professionals can significantly—sometimes exponentially—grow their businesses. For example, the wealthy are steadily choosing family office practices over other types of providers. Being able to establish and methodically grow a high-performing family office practice results in greater value to high-net-worth individuals and families and considerably more success for the professionals.

At the same time, a large percentage of the wealthy, for various reasons, are being poorly served by the professionals they rely on. Many of the wealthy, for example, are working with pretenders—professionals who want to do a good job but are not up to the task. We provide educational resources to correct this and other failures so the wealthy can make smarter financial and lifestyle decisions.

Research insights coupled with more than three decades of experience working with leading professionals and the wealthy, including the super-rich, produce actionable processes and solutions that can make a significant difference quickly.